RELIGION IN AMERICAN LIFE

Conrad Wright

HOUGHTON
★ MIFFLIN ★
HISTORY
PROGRAM

★★★

■ *Life in America Series*

General *editor:* **Richard C. Wade**

HOUGHTON MIFFLIN COMPANY / *Boston*

RELIGION IN AMERICAN LIFE

Selected Readings

CONRAD WRIGHT

Harvard University

New York / Atlanta / Geneva, Ill. / Dallas / Palo Alto

■ *About the Author and Editor*

CONRAD WRIGHT

Professor of American Church History at the Harvard Divinity School, Dr. Wright previously taught in the Humanities Department at the Massachusetts Institute of Technology. He is the author of The Beginnings of Unitarianism in America and The Liberal Christians, as well as numerous articles in professional and scholarly journals.

RICHARD C. WADE

General editor for the LIFE IN AMERICA series, Dr. Wade is Professor of American History at the City University of New York. He is the author of Slavery in the Cities and The Urban Frontier.

Copyright © 1972 by Houghton Mifflin Company

All rights reserved. No part of this work may be reproduced or transmitted in any form or by any means, electronic or mechanical, including photocopying and recording, or by any information storage or retrieval system, without permission in writing from the publisher.

Printed in the United States of America

Library of Congress Catalog Card Number: 72–180481

ISBN: 0–395–03145–1

■ *Contents*

■ *Life in America Series*

More than a half century ago the philosopher George Santayana, writing about his fellow Americans in *Character and Opinion in the United States,* had this to say:

> . . . if there are immense differences between individual Americans . . . yet there is a great uniformity in their environment, customs, temper, and thoughts. They have all been uprooted from their several soils and ancestries and plunged together into one vortex, whirling irresistibly in a space otherwise quite empty. To be an American is of itself a moral condition, an educaton, and a career. . . .

One might express this idea another way by saying that there is indeed broad diversity in American life and yet enough similarity in the American experience to enable us profitably to explore that experience in its various facets — whether we are speaking of its rich cultural heritage or of the development of its political and social institutions. For "this soil is propitious to every seed," wrote Santayana. And it will be the purpose of the LIFE IN AMERICA series — of which the present volume is one — to trace the planting and the growth of those many seeds that go to make up American civilization as we know it today.

Coming originally from different — often disparate — national and social backgrounds, speaking a multiplicity of languages, our colonial forbears found on this broad continent the room and the freedom they sought. Here they shaped a new society while yet preserving much of their older heritage. From this interaction between the old and new, between the land and the people, a distinctively American civilization emerged.

For nearly two hundred years the mainstream of American life has remained sufficiently broad and open to contain a great variety of views and experience while continuing to add to — and thereby to enrich — our total cultural heritage.

This series examines what has come to be known as the American way of life by looking into the separate aspects of the American experience. It emphasizes not only the crises in the American past but traces the continuities as well. It discovers meaning in the life of ordinary people as well as in the achievements of their leaders. It illumines the great movements of history by viewing them first hand through the eyes of contemporaries. Most of all, it puts the student on the stage of history, making him a companion of the generations and the groups that have gone before.

Each volume in the LIFE IN AMERICA series relates the experience of a single group. One group will be distinguished by its common background; others by nationality, race, or occupation. In each, the story will begin by examining the way in which the given group has become a part of the American story. Other selections will trace their development, chronicle their troubles and achievements and, finally, suggest present problems and prospects.

In this way the student will receive a balanced picture of the growth of his country. Instead of seeing American history as a series of crises and conflicts only, he will perceive also the continuing, if sometimes uneven, development of a free society. Instead of trying to find in Washington all the keys to understanding the American achievement, he will be encouraged to seek them as well in the many other sections of the country. And in searching for the significance of events, he will focus his attention not only on the prominent figures of history but on the experiences of ordinary citizens as well. He will be invited to participate vicariously, as he reads, in their struggles, hopes, aspirations, failures, and successes.

The present volume traces the development of American religion from the earliest colonial experience to the present. The men and women who came to America held a variety of religious convictions. Encouraged by an atmosphere of freedom and tolerance, their beliefs grew and were redefined in American terms. The story of this religious development is told here almost completely in the words of the participants. The readings have been reproduced as they appeared in the original sources, save that in certain instances paragraph indentations have been added, the punctuation altered, italics removed, and obscure words defined, in order to facilitate comprehension.

Part One

Religion in Colonial America

Part One: Introduction

When European travelers came to this country, in the mid-nineteenth century especially, one of the things they remarked over and over again was the number and variety of American religious denominations. Instead of one dominant church officially recognized by the state — Anglican in England, Lutheran in much of Germany, Catholic in countries like Italy — they found all denominations standing on common ground and relying on voluntary contributions rather than state support. The policy of separation of church and state, and the fact of religious pluralism, were evidently closely related.

While the selections in this book have not been chosen with an eye exclusively to this interrelation between pluralism and the separation of church and state, this is nevertheless the most obvious recurrent theme to be found in them.

Colonial America

A number of the colonies that were afterwards joined to form the United States were at the outset religiously very homogeneous. New England was Puritan, Virginia was Anglican. Yet there was diversity from the beginning in Maryland and Pennsylvania; and the colonies taken as a whole included many different religious groups. The story of religion in colonial America has as a central theme a slowly increasing pluralism, punctuated (in the Great Awakening) by an episode of crisis and rapid change. ■

I. Errand into the Wilderness

What drove, or drew, thousands of Englishmen in the seventeenth century to hazard the Atlantic crossing and establish colonies in the Western World? The motives were varied, and often mixed. The lure of adventure attracted some, the opportunity for economic gain attracted others. Some sought escape from religious persecution, or had more or less clearly in mind the blueprint for a holy commonwealth they hoped to construct. The selections that follow indicate some of the ways in which religious motivations were involved in this migration of peoples. Yet it should be remembered that even those for whom economic factors loomed largest could not avoid the common religious presuppositions of the day. Even the most secular of events, therefore, could be given a theological interpretation, and be understood in the context of the unceasing conflict between the powers of light and the powers of darkness. Whether this conflict took place within the individual soul, or in the events of history, it was a real battle, though one in which God's purposes could not ultimately be frustrated. ■

1. Queen Elizabeth Urged to Colonize America[1]

✛ Richard Hakluyt

Sir Walter Raleigh is remembered both as a courtier of Queen Elizabeth and as a promoter of colonization in America. In 1584, at his request, a young clergyman named Richard Hakluyt prepared a lengthy treatise, explaining the reasons why the English government should adopt a policy of colonization in America. While much attention is given to economic factors, and to strategic advantages in the conflict with Spain, it is interesting to note that first place is given to the conversion of the natives.

[1] Text with modernized spelling from Richard Hakluyt, A *Discourse on Western Planting.* (*Collections of the Maine Historical Society,* 2nd Series, Vol. II, pp. 7–12.)

3

Hakluyt is best remembered today for his compilation of accounts of voyages of discovery, entitled The Principal Navigations, Voyages, Traffiques and Discoveries of the English Nation. ■

Seeing that the people of that part of America from 30 degrees in Florida northward unto 63 degrees (which is yet in no Christian prince's actual possession) are idolaters, . . . it remaineth to be thoroughly weighed and considered by what means and by whom this most godly and Christian work may be performed of enlarging the glorious gospel of Christ, and reducing of infinite multitudes of these simple people that are in error into the right and perfect way of their salvation. . . . Now the kings and queens of England have the name of Defenders of the Faith. By which title I think they are not only charged to maintain and patronize the faith of Christ, but also to enlarge and advance the same. Neither ought this to be their last work, but rather the principal and chief of all others, according to the commandment of our Saviour, Christ: First seek the kingdom of God and the righteousness thereof, and all other things shall be ministered unto you (Matthew 6).

Now the means to send such as shall labor effectually in this business is by planting one or two colonies of our nation upon that firm,[2] where they may remain in safety, and first learn the language of the people near adjoining (the gift of tongues being now taken away), and by little and little acquaint themselves with their manner, and so with discretion and mildness distill into their purged minds the sweet and lively liquor of the gospel. . . .

And this enterprise the princes of the religion (among whom Her Majesty is principal) ought the rather to take in hand, because the papists confirm themselves and draw others to their side, showing that they are the true Catholic church because they have been the only converters of many millions of infidels to Christianity. Yea, I myself have been demanded of them how many infidels have been by us converted. . . . Now therefore I trust the time is at hand when by Her Majesty's forwardness in this enterprise not only this objection and such like shall be answered by our fruitful labor in God's harvest among the infidels, but also many inconveniences and strifes amongst ourselves at home in matters of ceremonies shall be ended.

[2] [firm: the mainland; compare the Latin phrase *terra firma*.]

2. Virginia Saved by God's Providence[1]

✤ William Crashaw

*Virginia was colonized by Englishmen seeking economic gain;
yet at the same time, they shared the religious and theological
presuppositions of the day. Hence they thought of themselves as
establishing a "Christian body politic" in the New World, and
understood events that we would regard as coincidences as the
direct intervention of God on their behalf. In the selection that
follows, such an interpretation is given to the fact that not a
single life was lost when a ship bound for Virginia was wrecked
on the island of Bermuda; and even more remarkable, to the
arrival of a rescue ship at Jamestown just as the colony was about
to be abandoned entirely.* ■

And this . . . is one of the four arguments, and as it were plain
demonstrations, that have convinced me to believe that assuredly God
himself is the founder, and favorer of this plantation. . . . I am of
mind, that the want either of knowledge, or consideration hereof,
hath been, and is the cause of the error and misprision [misunder-
standing] of the world, touching this business; and do think that if
men did ruminate, and advisedly consider of these particulars, they
would reprove themselves for their former thoughts, and say plainly,
Digitus Dei est hic.[2]

1. The marvelous and indeed miraculous deliverance of our worthy
governors, Sir Thomas Gates, Lieutenant General, and Sir George
Somers, Admiral, with all their company, of some hundred and fifty
persons, upon the feared and abhorred islands of the Bermudas, without loss of one person, when the same hour nothing was before their
eyes, but imminent and inevitable death; as never ship came there
that perished not, so never was it heard of, that any ship wrecked
there, but with the death of all or most of the people, save only this
of ours. . . .

2. The full discovery (by means of their former deliverance) of

¹ Text with modernized spelling from William Crashaw, "The Epistle Dedi-
catorie," prefixed to Alexander Whitaker, *Good Newes from Virginia* (London:
William Welby, 1613), pp. A4 (v)–B1 (r).
² [**Digitus Dei est hic:** this is the finger of God.]

those Bermuda Islands, which hitherto have been held in the world as inaccessible, so not habitable, but so fearful, hideous and hateful, as it seemed a place abandoned of God and man, and given up to the devil's power and possession, and to be of all known places in the world a very hell upon earth, rather than a place for men to dwell in. . . .

3. The special and most fatherly providence of God over this action, in upholding it when man had forsaken it, and giving it life again when man had left it for dead. For had not Sir Thomas Gates and Sir George Somers come into Virginia from the Bermudas even when they did, the poor colony (which during that year of their absence, by enduring the misery of misgovernment, had fallen into all extremity of distress) had been gone away, and our plantation possessed by the savages; and (which was much more miraculous) when they being come in, and in all about 240 persons, and in such extreme misery and famine, as the Honorable Commander was even forced to yield to that which others moved (but himself had rather have died than done) — namely, to put themselves to the sea to come for England, and quit the country. And when this (full sore against his heart) and put in execution, and every man aboard, their ordnance and armor buried, and not an English soul left in James Town, and giving by their peal of shot their last and woeful farewell to that pleasant land, were now with sorrowful hearts going down the river, behold the hand of heaven from above, at the very instant, sent in the Right Honorable La Warr[3] to meet them even at the river's mouth, with provision and comforts of all kind, who if he had stayed but two tides longer had come into Virginia and not found one English man. Whereupon they all with as much joy returned, as with sorrow they had come away, and making as it were a new entry and possession, took up their ordnance and their armor and the next day received their Honorable Lord General with all joy and applause. And from that day by God's blessing they never wanted government, they never wanted bread, for him that would take pains and do his duty. If ever the hand of God appeared in action of man, it was here most evident, for when man had forsaken this business, God took it in hand; and when men said, now hath all the earth cast off the

---

[3] [**La Warr:** Baron De La Warr, for whom Delaware was named.]

care of this plantation, the hand of heaven hath taken hold of it. God therefore be glorified in his own work.

3. The Pilgrims Seek Refuge from Persecution[1]
✤ William Bradford

The Pilgrims were fewer in numbers than the Massachusetts Bay Puritans, and of humbler origins, but the story of their migration is a much more familiar part of the American tradition. The reason is partly their example of steadfast religious faith amidst adversity, and partly the literary quality of the historical account of their settlement by Governor Bradford, from which this selection is taken. ■

Persecution in England

When as by the travail and diligence of some godly and zealous preachers and God's blessing on their labors, as in other places of the land so in the North parts, many became enlightened by the word of God and had their ignorance and sins discovered unto them and began by his grace to reform their lives and make conscience of their ways, the work of God was no sooner manifest in them than presently they were both scoffed and scorned by the profane multitude, and the ministers urged with the yoke of subscription or else must be silenced. And the poor people were so vexed with apparitors and pursuivants[2] and the commissary courts as truly their affliction was not small. Which, notwithstanding, they bore sundry years with much patience, till they were occasioned by the continuance and increase of these troubles and other means which the Lord raised up in those days to see further into things by the light of the word of God. How not only these base and beggarly ceremonies were unlawful, but

---

[1] William Bradford, *Of Plymouth Plantation*, in *Collections of the Massachusetts Historical Society*, vol. III of the Fourth Series (Boston: Little, Brown and Company, 1856), pp. 8, 22, 23–24, 58–59.

[2] [**apparitors and pursuivants:** English officials whose duty was to enforce religious conformity.]

also that the lordly and tyrannous power of the prelates ought not to be submitted unto; which thus, contrary to the freedom of the gospel, would load and burden men's consciences, and by their compulsive power make a profane mixture of persons and things in the worship of God. And that their offices and callings, courts and canons, etc., were unlawful and antichristian, being such as have no warrant in the word of God. . . .

So many, therefore, of these professors as saw the evil of these things in these parts, and whose hearts the Lord had touched with heavenly zeal for his truth, they shook off this yoke of antichristian bondage, and as the Lord's free people joined themselves by a covenant of the Lord into a church estate, in the fellowship of the gospel, to walk in all his ways made known or to be made known unto them, according to their best endeavors, whatsoever it should cost them, the Lord assisting them. And that it cost them something this ensuing history will declare. . . .

The Decision to Leave Holland

After they had lived in this city[3] about some eleven or twelve years . . . and sundry of them were taken away by death and many others began to be well stricken in years (the grave mistress of Experience having taught them many things), those prudent governors with sundry of the sagest members began both deeply to apprehend their present dangers and wisely to foresee the future and think of timely remedy. In the agitation of their thoughts and much discourse of things hereabout, at length they began to incline to this conclusion: of removal to some other place. Not out of any newfangledness or other such like giddy humor by which men are oftentimes transported to their great hurt and danger, but for sundry weighty and solid reasons, some of the chief of which I will here briefly touch.

And first, they saw and found by experience the hardness of the place and country to be such as few in comparison would come to them, and fewer that would bide it out and continue with them. For many that came to them, and many more that desired to be with them, could not endure that great labor and hard fare with other inconveniences which they underwent and were contented with. . . .

[3] [this city: Leyden]

Secondly. They saw that though the people generally bore all these difficulties very cheerfully and with a resolute courage, being in the best and strength of their years, yet old age began to steal on many of them; and their great and continual labors with other crosses and sorrows, hastened it before the time. So as it was not only probably thought, but apparently seen, that within a few years more they would be in danger to scatter by necessities pressing them, or sink under their burdens, or both. . . .

Thirdly. As necessity was a taskmaster over them so they were forced to be such, not only to their servants but in a sort to their dearest children, the which as it did not a little wound the tender hearts of many a loving father and mother, so it produced likewise sundry sad and sorrowful effects. For many of their children that were of best dispositions and gracious inclinations, having learned to bear the yoke in their youth and willing to bear part of their parents' burden, were oftentimes so oppressed with their heavy labors that though their minds were free and willing, yet their bodies bowed under the weight of the same, and became decrepit in their early youth, the vigor of nature being consumed in the very bud as it were. But that which was more lamentable, and of all sorrows most heavy to be borne, was that many of their children, by these occasions and the great licentiousness of youth in that country and the manifold temptations of the place, were drawn away by evil examples into extravagant and dangerous courses, getting the reins off their necks and departing from their parents. Some became soldiers, others took upon them far voyages by sea, and others some worse courses tending to dissoluteness and the danger of their souls, to the great grief of their parents and dishonor of God. So that they saw their posterity would be in danger to degenerate and be corrupted.

Lastly (and which was not least), a great hope and inward zeal they had of laying some good foundation, or at least to make some way thereunto, for the propagating and advancing the gospel of the kingdom of Christ in those remote parts of the world; yea, though they should be but even as steppingstones unto others for the performing of so great a work.

These and some other like reasons moved them to undertake this resolution of their removal; the which they afterward prosecuted with so great difficulties, as by the sequel will appear. . . .

The Departure for America

At length, after much travel and these debates, all things were got ready and provided. A small ship [the *Speedwell*] was bought and fitted in Holland, which was intended as to serve to help to transport them, so to stay in the country and attend upon fishing and such other affairs as might be for the good and benefit of the colony when they came there. Another was hired at London, of burden about 9 score [the *Mayflower*], and all other things got in readiness. So being ready to depart, they had a day of solemn humiliation, their pastor taking his text from Ezra viii.21: "And there at the river, by Ahava, I proclaimed a fast, that we might humble ourselves before our God, and seek of him a right way for us, and for our children, and for all our substance." Upon which he spent a good part of the day very profitably and suitable to their present occasion; the rest of the time was spent in pouring out prayers to the Lord with great fervency, mixed with abundance of tears. And the time being come that they must depart, they were accompanied with most of their brethren out of the city, unto a town sundry miles off called Delftshaven, where the ship lay ready to receive them. So they left that goodly and pleasant city which had been their resting place near twelve years; but they knew they were pilgrims, and looked not much on those things, but lift[ed] up their eyes to the heavens, their dearest country, and quieted their spirits. . . .

Arrival in New England

Being thus arrived in a good harbor, and brought safe to land, they fell upon their knees and blessed the God of Heaven who had brought them over the vast and furious ocean and delivered them from all the perils and miseries thereof, again to set their feet on the firm and stable earth, their proper element. And no marvel if they were thus joyful, seeing wise Seneca was so affected with sailing a few miles on the coast of his own Italy, as he affirmed, that he had rather remain twenty years on his way by land than pass by sea to any place in a short time, so tedious and dreadful was the same unto him.

But here I cannot but stay and make a pause, and stand half amazed at this poor people's present condition; and so I think will the reader, too, when he well considers the same. [Having] thus passed the vast ocean and a sea of troubles before in their preparation (as may be remembered by that which went before), they had now no friends to welcome them nor inns to entertain or refresh their weatherbeaten bodies; no houses or much less towns to repair to, to seek for succor. It is recorded in Scripture as a mercy to the Apostle and his shipwrecked company that the barbarians showed them no small kindness in refreshing them; but these savage barbarians, when they met with them (as after will appear), were readier to fill their sides full of arrows than otherwise. And for the season it was winter, and they that know the winters of that country know them to be sharp and violent, and subject to cruel and fierce storms, dangerous to travel to known places, much more to search an unknown coast. Besides, what could they see but a hideous and desolate wilderness, full of wild beasts and wild men — and what multitudes there might be of them they knew not. Neither could they, as it were, go up to the top of [Mount] Pisgah to view from this wilderness a more goodly country to feed their hopes; for which way soever they turned their eyes (save upward to the heavens) they could have little solace or content in respect of any outward objects. For summer being done, all things stand upon them with a weatherbeaten face, and the whole country, full of woods and thickets, represented a wild and savage hue. If they looked behind them, there was the mighty ocean which they had passed and was now as a main bar and gulf to separate them from all the civil parts of the world. . . .

What could now sustain them but the Spirit of God and his grace? May not and ought not the children of these fathers rightly say: "Our fathers were Englishmen which came over this great ocean, and were ready to perish in this wilderness; but they cried unto the Lord, and he heard their voice and looked on their adversity," etc. "Let them therefore praise the Lord, because he is good: and his mercies endure forever." "Yea, let them which have been redeemed of the Lord, shew how he hath delivered them from the hand of the oppressor. When they wandered in the desert wilderness out of the way, and found no city to dwell in, both hungry and thirsty, their soul was overwhelmed in them. Let them confess before the Lord his lovingkindness and his wonderful works before the sons of men."

4. New England Congregationalism[1]

✤ Thomas Lechford

Both the Pilgrims at Plymouth and the Puritans of Massachu-
setts Bay insisted that government of the Church by bishops and
archbishops was unscriptural. Each particular church or congre-
gation, they said, has full power to order its own affairs, though
at the same time all should walk harmoniously together. Congre-
gationalism depended on the participation of all adult members,
and so ultimately developed into a democratic form of govern-
ment, even though at the beginning the officers of the churches
exercised a rather autocratic rule. The description that follows is
by an English lawyer who visited Massachusetts Bay in 1638, but
who left in 1641 because he found he was not really in sympathy
with the leaders of the colony. ■

A church is gathered there after this manner: A convenient, or
competent number of Christians, allowed by the General Court[2] to
plant together, at a day prefixed, come together in public manner
in some fit place, and there confess their sins and profess their faith
one unto another, and being satisfied of one another's faith and
repentance, they solemnly enter into a covenant with God and one
another (which is called their church covenant, and held by them to
constitute a church) to this effect: *viz.*,

To forsake the Devil and all his works and the vanities of the
sinful world, and all their former lusts and corruptions they have lived
and walked in, and to cleave unto and obey the Lord Jesus Christ as
their only king and lawgiver, their only priest and prophet, and to
walk together with that church, in the unity of the faith and brotherly
love, and to submit themselves one unto another in all the ordinances
of Christ, to mutual edification and comfort, to watch over and support one another.

Whereby they are called the church of such a place, which before

---

[1] Text with modernized spelling from Thomas Lechford, *Plain Dealing, or*
News from New England (Boston: J. K. Wiggin and Wm. Parsons Lunt, 1867),
pp. 12–16.

[2] [**General Court:** the governing body of the colony, exercising both legislative
and judicial functions.]

they say were no church, nor of any church except the invisible. After this, they do at the same time or some other, all being together, elect their own officers, as pastor, teacher, elders, deacons, if they have fit men enough to supply those places; else, as many of them as they can be provided of.

Then they set another day for the ordination of their said officers, and appoint some of themselves to impose hands upon their officers, which is done in a public day of fasting and prayer. Where there are ministers or elders before, they impose their hands upon the new officers, but where there is none, there some of their chiefest men, two or three of good report amongst them, though not of the ministry, do, by appointment of the said church, lay hands upon them. And after the said ordination, if there are any elders of other churches present (as of late I have known divers have been present under the names of the messengers of the churches), they give the new officers the right hand of fellowship, taking them by the right hand, every one severally, or else sometimes one foreign elder in the name of all the rest, gives the right hand of fellowship with a set speech unto them. . . . And at the planting of a church or gathering, as they term it, one of the church messengers of foreign churches examines and tries the men to be molded into a church, discerns their faith and repentance, and their covenant being before ready made, written, subscribed, and here read and acknowledged, he discerns and pronounceth them to be a true church of Christ, and gives them the right hand of fellowship, and all this in the name of Christ and of all the church messengers present and their churches. . . .

And the General Court will not allow of any church otherwise gathered.

5. Religious Toleration in Maryland[1]

✤ *Report of Court Action, 1638*

Maryland was settled in 1634 by the Calverts, a Roman Catholic family, in order to establish both a landed estate for themselves and a place where their coreligionists might settle. Realizing that a purely Catholic colony would be impossible, Cecil

---

[1] Text with modernized spelling from *Archives of Maryland* (Baltimore: Maryland Historical Society, 1887), Vol. IV, pp. 37–38.

*Calvert prepared instructions to the governor that religious con-
troversy should be excluded, so that Protestants and Catholics
might live together in peace. The following report of a court
case shows how these instructions were enforced. Even though
later developments in Maryland compromised the principle of
religious toleration, the Calverts deserve credit for practicing it at
a time when an insistence on religious conformity was the general
rule.* ■

Then were the complaints contained in the writing against William
Lewis taken into examination. And touching the first, Ellis Beach
did depose that William Lewis coming into the room where Francis
Gray and Robert Sedgrave were reading of Mr. Smith's sermons,
William Lewis said that the book was made by the instrument of
the devil. . . . And William Lewis being put to his answer confessed
that coming into the room where they were reading of a book, they
read it aloud to the end he should hear it, and that the matter being
much reproachful to his religion, namely, that the Pope was Anti-
christ, and the Jesuits, antichristian ministers, etc., he told them that
it was a falsehood, and came from the devil, as all lies did, and that
he that writ it was an instrument of the devil. . . .

Touching the second, it was deposed by two witnesses that William
Lewis said that their ministers (innuendo the Protestants) were the
ministers of the devil.

Touching the third, Robert Sedgrave said at first that William
Lewis did forbid them to use or have any Protestant books within his
house; which being denied by William Lewis, and that he had
expressly given them leave to use or have books, so they read them
not to his offence or disturbance in his own house; and that he spake
only touching that book then in reading. Robert Sedgrave said that
he was not certain whether he forbade them that book only, or all
other books. . . .

The Sentence of the Court

And Mr. Secretary found him guilty of an offensive and indiscreet
speech in calling the author of the book an instrument of the devil;
but acquitted him from that he was charged withal in the writing,
that he used that speech touching Protestant ministers in general.
He likewise found him guilty of a very offensive speech in calling the

Protestant ministers the ministers of the devil. He likewise found him
to have exceeded in forbidding them to read a book otherwise allowed
and lawful to be read by the state of England; but he acquitted him
of the accusation that he forbade his servants to have or use Protestant books in his house. And because these his offensive speeches,
and other [of] his unseasonable disputations in point of religion
tended to the disturbance of the public peace and quiet of the colony,
and were committed by him against a public proclamation set forth
to prohibit all such disputes, therefore he fined him in five-hundred-
weight of tobacco to the lord of the province, and to remain in the
sheriff's custody until he found sufficient sureties for his good behavior in those kinds in time to come.

6. Religious Pluralism in Pennsylvania[1]

✣ Francis Daniel Pastorius

*The experiment of religious diversity and mutual forbearance
attempted by the Calverts was tried again a half-century later by
William Penn under more advantageous circumstances. Penn's
colony attracted English, Scotch Irish, German, and Dutch
settlers, who brought with them Quakerism, the Church of
England, Presbyterianism, Lutheranism, German Reformed (Calvinist) Churches, and many varieties of German sectarianism.
Francis Pastorius, the author of the following description of religious pluralism in Pennsylvania in 1700, was a German Quaker
of Lutheran background. He founded Germantown in 1683.* ■

William Penn's Laws

Firstly, no one shall be disturbed on account of his belief, but
freedom of conscience shall be granted to all inhabitants of the
province, so that every nation may build and conduct churches according to their desires.

2. Sunday shall be consecrated to the public worship of God. The

[1] Francis D. Pastorius, "Circumstantial Geographical Description of Pennsyl-
vania," adapted from Albert Cook Myers, ed., *Narratives of Early Pennsylvania,
West New Jersey, and Delaware, 1630–1707*, pp. 379, 384–388. Barnes & Noble
Publishers, New York, New York.

teaching of God shall be so zealously carried on that its purity can be recognized in each listener from the fruits which arise from it.

Religion of the Indians

They know of no idols, but they worship a single all-powerful and merciful God, who limits the power of the Devil. They also believe in the immortality of the soul, which, after the course of life is finished, has a suitable recompense from the all-powerful hand of God awaiting it. . . .

They listen very willingly, and not without perceptible emotion, to discourse concerning the Creator of heaven and earth, and his divine light, which enlightens all men who have come into the world and who are yet to be born, and concerning the wisdom and love of God, because of which he gave his only-begotten and most dearly-beloved son to die for us. It is only to be regretted that we cannot yet speak their language readily, and therefore cannot set forth to them the thoughts and intent of our own hearts, namely, how great a power and salvation lies concealed in Christ Jesus. They are very quiet and thoughtful in our gatherings, so that I fully believe that in the future, at the great day of judgment, they will come forth with those of Tyre and Sidon, and put to shame many thousands of false nominal and canting Christians.

Religious Groups in the Province

The native naked inhabitants have no written articles of belief, since no traces can be found that any Christian teachers have ever come among them. They only know their native language by means of which the parents instruct their children through tradition, and teach them that which they have heard of and learned from their parents.

2. The English and Dutch are for the most part adherents of the Calvinist religion.

3. The Quakers are known in Philadelphia, through William Penn.

4. The Swedes and High Germans are Evangelical. They have their own church, whose minister is named Fabricius, of whom I must declare with sorrow that he is much addicted to drink, and is well-nigh blind in the inner man.[2]

---

[2] [blind in the inner man: lacking in inner religious experience. As a Quaker, Pastorius was critical of what he considered the external formalism of other groups.]

THE COLONIAL HERITAGE: The colonies were first settled largely for religious reasons. The church long served as the focal point for the social and spiritual activities of the colonists. The lofty pulpit and long sermon were characteristic features of Puritan worship (right). The Salem witchcraft trials attested to the high degree of religious conformity in the early Puritan communities. Below is a nineteenth century view of the trial of George Jacobs in 1692. (Painting by Tompkins H. Matteson, 1855.)

William Penn, founder of the Province of Pennsylvania, is known for his practical application of the principle of religious freedom and for his humane treatment of the Indians. Below is Benjamin West's painting depicting Penn's 1681 treaty with the Indians at Shackamaxon, Pennsylvania.

Here in Germanton, in the year 1686, we built a little church for the community, but did not have as our aim an outwardly great stone edifice, but rather that the temple of God which we believers constitute should be built up, and that we ourselves should be, all together, holy and unspotted.

The Evangelical ministers could have had a fine opportunity here to carry out the command of Christ — Go forth throughout the world and preach the gospel — if they had preferred to be followers of Christ rather than servants of their bodies, and if they had been devoted to the inner theology rather than to verbal discourse.

II. Times of Transition and Tribulation

Whether they were drawn by the lure of adventure, or the dream of a theocratic society, or economic opportunity, the first settlers were engaged in the construction of institutions of church and state where none had existed before. Their children, however, could take for granted the social institutions the fathers had labored to construct. This fact alone would have produced a subtle change in attitudes. But at the same time, the rise of modern science was transforming the mind of the West, and altering the presuppositions within which the religious life was to be experienced and interpreted. Orthodox religious doctrines came to be questioned, and religious institutions did not seem to be working as they were supposed to do. Accepted landmarks were disappearing; and once confident people were becoming worried and confused. ■

1. A Puritan Condemns a Wayward Generation[1]

✣ Samuel Danforth

New England was founded by Puritans as a city on a hill, which should be a shining example to all the Protestant world. It was intended to demonstrate that churches could be organized on a congregational basis without producing chaos and schism; that church and state could co-operate without either one's interfering in the proper activities of the other; that the revealed will of God could be made the established rule even in the affairs of sinful men. But the religious fervor of the founding generation, which for a time made this audacious program plausible, could not be maintained by the generations that followed. Before long, laments were heard that New England was faithless to her trust. Times were changing; Puritan was becoming Yankee; this-worldly concerns were coming increasingly to the fore. ■

[1] Samuel Danforth, A Brief Recognition of New-England's Errand into the Wilderness (Cambridge: S. Green and M. Johnson, 1671), pp. 9–13.

19

Of solemn and serious enquiry to us all in this general assembly, is whether we have not in a great measure forgotten our errand into the wilderness. You have solemnly professed before God, angels, and men, that the cause of your leaving your country, kindred, and fathers' houses, and transporting yourselves with your wives, little ones, and substance over the vast ocean into this waste and howling wilderness, was your liberty to walk in the faith of the gospel with all good conscience according to the order of the gospel, and your enjoyment of the pure worship of God according to his institution, without human mixtures and impositions. Now let us sadly consider whether our ancient and primitive affections to the Lord Jesus, his glorious gospel, his pure and spiritual worship, and the order of his house, remain, abide, and continue firm, constant, entire, and inviolate. . . .

In our first and best times the kingdom of heaven brake in upon us with a holy violence, and every man pressed into it. What mighty efficacy and power had the clear and faithful dispensation of the Gospel upon your hearts! How affectionately and zealously did you entertain the kingdom of God! How careful were you, even all sorts, young and old, high and low, to take hold of the opportunities of your spiritual good and edification, ordering your secular affairs (which were wreathed and twisted together with great variety) so as not to interfere with your general calling, but that you might attend upon the Lord without distraction! . . . What earnest and ardent desires had you in those days after communion with Christ in the holy sacraments! . . . What pious care was there of sister churches, that those that wanted breasts might be supplied, and that those that wanted peace, their dissensions might be healed! . . . What holy endeavors were there in those days to propagate religion to your children and posterity, training them up in the nurture and admonition of the Lord, keeping them under the awe of government, restraining their enormities and extravagancies, charging them to know the God of their fathers and serve him with a perfect heart and willing mind, and publicly asserting and maintaining their interest in the Lord and in his holy covenant and zealously opposing those that denied the same! . . .

But who is there left among you that saw these churches in their first glory and how do you see them now? Are they not in your eyes in comparison thereof as nothing? "How is the gold become dim!

how is the most fine gold changed!"[2] Is not the temper, complexion, and countenance of the churches strangely altered? Doth not a careless, remiss, flat, dry, cold, dead frame of spirit grow in upon us secretly, strongly, prodigiously? They that have ordinances are as though they had none; and they that hear the Word as though they heard it not; and they that pray as though they prayed not; and they that receive sacraments as though they received them not; and they that are exercised in the holy things, using them by the by as matters of custom and ceremony, so as not to hinder their eager prosecution of other things which their hearts are set upon. . . . Pride, contention, worldliness, covetousness, luxury, drunkenness, and uncleanness break in like a flood upon us and good men grow cold in their love to God and to one another.

[2] Lamentations 4, 1.

2. Wonders of the Invisible World[1]
✢ Cotton Mather

The witchcraft episode that distracted Salem Village in 1692 has bothered scholars ever since. Does it demonstrate that the Puritans were superstitious bigots? Are the ministers to be blamed for whipping up the excitement that caused the death of a score of innocent men and women? A crucial document bearing on the matter is the response to a request for advice from the Governor of the Province of Massachusetts Bay, prepared by Cotton Mather on behalf of a group of ministers. It does take for granted the prevailing belief in witchcraft. But it also questions a reliance on "spectral evidence" — that is, the assertion by a victim of witchcraft that he had seen the specter (ghost) of the accused witch tormenting him. Since such spectral evidence had been crucial in trials for witchcraft, to declare it to be unreliable was to cut the heart out of the cases against the accused. And witchcraft for which there was no acceptable evidence was on its way to being rejected altogether. ■

[1] Text reprinted from the "Postscript" to Increase Mather, *Cases of Conscience Concerning Evil Spirits Personating Men* (London: John Dunton, 1693).

I. The afflicted state of our poor neighbors, that are now suffering by molestations from the invisible world, we apprehend so deplorable, that we think their condition calls for the utmost help of all persons in their several capacities.

II. We cannot but with all thankfulness acknowledge the success which the merciful God has given unto the sedulous and assiduous endeavors of our honorable rulers, to detect the abominable witchcrafts which have been committed in the country, humbly praying that the discovery of these mysterious and mischievous wickednesses may be perfected.

III. We judge that in the prosecution of these, and all such witchcrafts, there is need of a very critical and exquisite caution, lest by too much credulity for things received only upon the Devil's authority, there be a door opened for a long train of miserable consequences, and Satan get an advantage over us, for we should not be ignorant of his devices.

IV. As in complaints upon witchcrafts, there may be matters of inquiry which do not amount unto matters of presumption, and there may be matters of presumption which yet may not be reckoned matters of conviction; so 'tis necessary that all proceedings thereabout be managed with an exceeding tenderness towards those that may be complained of, especially if they have been persons formerly of an unblemished reputation.

V. When the first inquiry is made into the circumstances of such as may lie under any just suspicion of witchcrafts, we could wish that there may be admitted as little as is possible of such noise, company, and openness, as may too hastily expose them that are examined, and that there may nothing be used as a test for the trial of the suspected, the lawfulness whereof may be doubted among the people of God; but that the directions given by such judicious writers as Perkins and Bernard,[2] be consulted in such a case.

VI. Presumptions whereupon persons may be committed, and much more convictions, whereupon persons may be condemned as guilty of witchcrafts, ought certainly to be more considerable than barely the accused persons being represented by a specter unto the afflicted, inasmuch as 'tis an undoubted and notorious thing that a

---

[2] [**Perkins and Bernard:** William Perkins and Richard Bernard were English Puritans who argued for great caution with respect to the evidence on which convictions for witchcraft were sought.]

demon may, by God's permission, appear even to ill purposes in the shape of an innocent, yea, and a virtuous man; nor can we esteem alterations made in the sufferers by a lock or touch of the accused to be an infallible evidence of guilt, but frequently liable to be abused by the Devil's legerdemains [trickery].

VII. We know not whether some remarkable affronts given to the devils by our disbelieving of those testimonies, whose whole force and strength is from them alone, may not put a period unto the progress of the dreadful calamity begun upon us in the accusation of so many persons, whereof we hope some are yet clear from the great transgression laid unto their charge.

VIII. Nevertheless, we cannot but humbly recommend unto the government the speedy and vigorous prosecution of such as have rendered themselves obnoxious, according to the direction given in the laws of God and the wholesome statutes of the English nation, for the detection of witchcrafts.

3. A Quaker Concern Regarding Slaveholding[1]

✢ Germantown Quakers, 1688

Black men were brought in bondage to Virginia in 1619, and from that time on, their experience has been part of American history. There has been disagreement among students as to the extent to which traditional African religious attitudes and practices survived the disruptive effect of enslavement and the Atlantic crossing. Authentic information from the point of view of those enslaved is hard to find. Easier to discover is the attitude of the white man, and the slow development of a moral and religious concern with respect to slavery. An early protest comes from Germantown Quakers, in 1688. ■

These are the reasons why we are against the traffic of men's bodies, as followeth: Is there any that would be done or handled at this manner, *viz.*, to be sold or made a slave for all the time of his

---

[1] Text with modernized spelling and punctuation from Samuel W. Pennypacker, "The Settlement of Germantown," *Pennsylvania Magazine of History and Biography*, IV (1880), pp. 28–30.

life? How fearful and fainthearted are many on sea when they see a strange vessel, being afraid it should be a Turk, and they should be taken and sold for slaves in Turkey. Now what is this better done as Turks do? Yea rather is it worse for them which say they are Christians, for we hear that the most part of such Negroes are brought hither against their will and consent, and that many of them are stolen. Now though they are black, we cannot conceive there is more liberty to have them slaves, as it is to have other white ones.

There is a saying that we shall do to all men like as we will be done ourselves, making no difference of what generation, descent, or color they are. And those who steal or rob men, and those who buy or purchase them, are they not all alike? Here is liberty of conscience, which is right and reasonable. Here ought to be likewise liberty of the body, except of evildoers, which is another case. But to bring men hither, or to rob and sell them against their will, we stand against. In Europe there are many oppressed for conscience sake, and here there are those oppressed which are of a black color. And we, who know that men must not commit adultery, some do commit adultery in others, separating wives from their husbands and giving them to others, and some sell the children of those poor creatures to other men.

Oh! do consider well this thing, you who do it, if you would be done at this manner, and if it is done according to Christianity! You surpass Holland and Germany in this thing. This makes an ill report in all those countries of Europe, where they hear that the Quakers do here handle men like they handle there the cattle; and for that reason some have no mind or inclination to come hither. And who shall maintain this your cause, or plead for it? Truly we cannot do so, except you shall inform us better hereof, *viz.*, that Christians have liberty to practice these things. Pray! what thing in the world can be done worse towards us than if men should rob or steal us away and sell us for slaves to strange countries, separating husband from his wife and children. Being now this is not done at that manner we will be done at, therefore we contradict and are against this traffic of men's bodies. . . .

This is from our meeting at Germantown, held the eighteenth of the second month, 1688, to be delivered to the monthly meeting at Richard Warrell's.

4. A Deist's Creed[1]

✤ Benjamin Franklin

A revolution in thought was produced by the rise of modern science. Occurrences that the Puritans would have attributed to the activity of spirits of the Invisible World were now explained in terms of uniform laws of nature. God was now thought of as revealed in the universal frame of nature as well as in a particular revelation such as may be found in the Bible. Some men, indeed, called "deists" or "freethinkers," argued that God's revelation of himself in nature made the notion of a particular revelation of his will superfluous. Benjamin Franklin was too urbane to ridicule believers in the Christian revelation, as some deists did. But his "Articles of Belief," prepared in 1728, show the influence on his religious ideas of the latest scientific model of a universe of heavenly bodies in harmonious motion. They also reflect a concern for human happiness in this world that contrasts with the old Puritan concern for eternal salvation in the next. ■

I believe there is one supreme, most perfect Being, author and father of the gods themselves. For I believe that man is not the most perfect being but one, rather that as there are many degrees of beings his inferiors, so there are many degrees of beings superior to him.

Also, when I stretch my imagination through and beyond our system of planets, beyond the visible fixed stars themselves, into that space that is every way infinite, and conceive it filled with suns like ours, each with a chorus of worlds forever moving round him, then this little ball on which we move seems even in my narrow imagination to be almost nothing, and myself less than nothing and of no sort of consequence.

When I think thus, I imagine it great vanity in me to suppose that the Supremely Perfect does in the least regard such an inconsiderable nothing as man. More especially, since it is impossible for me to have any positive clear idea of that which is infinite and incomprehensible, I cannot conceive otherwise than that he, the Infinite Father, expects

[1] Benjamin Franklin, "Articles of Belief," in *Writings*, ed. A. H. Smyth (New York: The Macmillan Company, 1905), Vol. III, pp. 92–94.

or requires no worship or praise from us, but that he is even infinitely above it.

But, since there is in all men something like a natural principle, which inclines them to devotion or the worship of some unseen power; and since men are endued with reason superior to all other animals that we are in our world acquainted with; therefore I think it seems required of me, and my duty as a man, to pay divine regards to *something*.

I conceive, then, that the Infinite has created many beings of gods vastly superior to man, who can better conceive his perfections than we, and return him a more rational and glorious praise. . . .

It may be that these created gods are immortal; or it may be that after many ages they are changed, and others supply their places.

Howbeit, I conceive that each of these is exceeding wise and good, and very powerful; and that each has made for himself one glorious sun, attended with a beautiful and admirable system of planets.

It is that particular wise and good God, who is the author and owner of our system, that I propose for the object of my praise and adoration. . . .

I conceive, for many reasons, that he is a good being; and as I should be happy to have so wise, good, and powerful a being my friend, let me consider in what manner I shall make myself most acceptable to him.

Next to the praise resulting from and due to his wisdom, I believe he is pleased and delights in the happiness of those he has created; and since without virtue man can have no happiness in this world, I firmly believe he delights to see me virtuous, because he is pleased when he sees me happy.

And since he has created many things which seem purely designed for the delight of man, I believe he is not offended when he sees his children solace themselves in any manner of pleasant exercises and innocent delights; and I think no pleasure innocent that is to man hurtful.

I *love* him therefore for his goodness, and I *adore* him for his wisdom.

Let me then not fail to praise my God continually, for it is his due, and it is all I can return for his many favors and great goodness to me, and let me resolve to be virtuous that I may be happy, that I may please him who is delighted to see me happy. Amen!

III. The Great Awakening

The eighteenth century was a time of striking countermovements in religion. On the one hand it produced Deism and other expressions of the spirit of reason in religion. But on the other hand, it fostered various movements emphasizing inward and emotional religious experience, such as Pietism and Methodism. In the American colonies, evangelical fervor of this kind found expression in the Great Awakening. This was a series of episodes of religious excitement that reached a climax in 1739–40 when George Whitefield, the great revivalist, traveled throughout the land from Georgia to Maine and back. The Awakening can be interpreted from various points of view; but one fruitful way of looking at it is to regard it as the result of the accumulated stresses and strains in the social institutions — especially the ecclesiastical institutions — established by the first settlers. Old institutions were breaking down as the population grew larger and more varied in outlook, and they had to be at least in part reconstructed. In New England, which had been most nearly homogeneous in population and uniform in religious culture, the "New Lights" who favored revivalistic methods were soon at odds with the "Old Lights" who opposed them, and churches began to split. Elsewhere revivalists discovered that they had a common concern for evangelical religion that cut across ethnic, or denominational, or geographical divisions. Once the ferment of the Awakening had broken apart old institutional structures, rapid theological change followed, as though new ideas had been too long held in restraint. Hence both in church organization and in doctrine, the Awakening was a major turning point for American religion. ■

1. Surprising Conversions in Northampton[1]

✤ Jonathan Edwards

Late in 1734, religious concern and interest was so stimulated in Northampton, Massachusetts, by a series of sermons by the Reverend Jonathan Edwards (1703–1750) that five or six persons were converted in a most remarkable way. Before long, the excitement was general throughout the town. Other conversions followed; and the revival spread to nearby towns. These events were the most spectacular instances of an awakening of religious concern prior to the arrival of George Whitefield in 1739–40. Edwards was convinced that the awakening was a glorious work of the Spirit of God, and he prepared for publication an account of what he had observed. ■

And then it was, in the latter part of December, that the Spirit of God began extraordinarily to set in, and wonderfully to work amongst us; and there were very suddenly, one after another, five or six persons who were, to all appearance, savingly converted, and some of them wrought upon in a very remarkable manner.

Particularly I was surprised with the relation of a young woman who had been one of the greatest company keepers in the whole town. When she came to me I had never heard that she was become in any wise serious, but by the conversation I then had with her, it appeared to me that what she gave an account of was a glorious work of God's infinite power and sovereign grace; and that God had given her a new heart, truly broken and sanctified. I could not then doubt of it, and have seen much in my acquaintance with her since to confirm it.

A Great Awakening Takes Place

Though the work was glorious, yet I was filled with concern about the effect it might have upon others. I was ready to conclude (though too rashly) that some would be hardened by it in careless and looseness of life; and would take occasion from it to open their mouths in reproaches of religion. But the event was the reverse to a wonderful

[1] Jonathan Edwards, "Narrative of Surprising Conversions," *Works* (New York: Leavitt, Trow & Co., 1844), Vol. III, pp. 234–35. (The italicized phrases in this selection are words Edwards quoted from the Bible.)

degree. God made it, I suppose, that greatest occasion of awakening to others of anything that ever came to pass in the town. I have had abundant opportunity to know the effect it had by my private conversation with many. The news of it seemed to be almost like a flash of lightning upon the hearts of young people all over the town, and upon many others. Those persons amongst us who used to be farthest from seriousness, and that I most feared would make an ill improvement of it, seemed greatly to be awakened with it. Many went to talk with her concerning what she had met with; and what appeared in her seemed to be to the satisfaction of all that did so.

Presently upon this, a great and earnest concern about the great things of religion and the eternal world became universal in all parts of the town and among persons of all degrees and all ages; the noise amongst the dry bones waxed louder and louder. All other talk but about spiritual and eternal things was soon thrown by. All the conversation in all companies and upon all occasions was upon these things only, unless so much as was necessary for people carrying on their ordinary secular business. Other discourse than of the things of religion would scarcely be tolerated in any company. The minds of people were wonderfully taken off from the world — it was treated amongst us as a thing of very little consequence. They seem to follow their worldly business more as a part of their duty than from any disposition they had to it. The temptation now seemed to lie on that hand to neglect worldly affairs too much, and to spend too much time in the immediate exercise of religion, which thing was exceedingly misrepresented by reports that were spread in distant parts of the land, as though the people here had wholly thrown by all worldly business, and betook themselves entirely to reading and praying and such like religious exercises.

Paramount Importance of Religion in Men's Minds

But though the people did not ordinarily neglect their worldly business, yet there then was the reverse of what commonly is. Religion was with all sorts the great concern, and the world was a thing only by the by. The only thing in their view was to get the kingdom of heaven, and every one appeared pressing into it. The engagedness of their hearts in this great concern could not be hid; it appeared in their very countenances. It then was a dreadful thing amongst us to lie out of Christ, in danger every day of dropping into hell; and what persons' minds were intent upon was to escape for their lives and to *fly from the wrath to come.* All would eagerly lay hold of opportunities for their souls, and were wont very often to meet together in private houses for religious purposes, and such meetings, when appointed, were wont greatly to be thronged.

There was scarcely a single person in the town, either old or young, that was left unconcerned about the great things of the eternal world. Those that were wont to be the vainest and loosest, and those that had been most disposed to think and speak slightly of vital and experimental religion, were now generally subject to great awakenings. And the work of conversion was carried on in a most astonishing manner, and increased more and more; souls did, as it were, come by flocks to Jesus Christ. From day to day, for many months together, might be seen evident instances of sinners brought *out of darkness into marvellous light,* and delivered *out of a horrible pit, and from the miry clay, and set upon a rock,* with a *new song of praise to God in their mouths.*

This work of God, as it was carried on, and the number of true saints multiplied, soon made a glorious alteration in the town; so that in the spring and summer following, [in the year] 1735, the town seemed to be full of the presence of God. It never was so full of love nor so full of joy and yet so full of distress as it was then. There were remarkable tokens of God's presence in almost every house. It was a time of joy in families on the account of salvation's being brought unto them; parents rejoicing over their children as new born, and husbands over their wives, and wives over their husbands. *The goings of God were then seen in his sanctuary, God's day was a delight, and his tabernacles were amiable.* Our public assemblies were then beautiful; the congregation was alive in God's service, everyone earnestly intent on the public worship, every hearer eager to drink in the words of the minister as they came from his mouth. The assembly in general were, from time to time, in tears while the word was preached, some weeping with sorrow and distress, others with joy and love, others with pity and concern for the souls of their neighbors.

THE GREAT AWAKENING: At the beginning of the eighteenth century some religious leaders feared that the piety and order of the earlier American churches was being threatened by increased population and intellectual diversity. Religion, they felt, was no longer the single unifying factor in American life. The Great Awakening, with its renewed emphasis on personal piety, countered some of these tendencies. It highlighted the importance of religion to the individual. Jonathan Edwards (right) laid the groundwork for this religious revival. The remarkable conversions at his church in Northampton, Massachusetts, are often considered the beginning of the Great Awakening.

The English evangelist preacher George Whitefield (below) preached throughout most of the American colonies, converting men and women of many denominations. He is often credited with breaking down the narrow, parochial character of the colonial churches.

2. Phebe Bartlett's Conversion[1]

Jonathan Edwards

Edwards included in his Narrative *an account of the conversion of Phebe Bartlett, who was then only four years old.* ∎

She was born in March, in the year 1731. About the latter end of April, or beginning of May, 1735, she was greatly affected by the talk of her brother, who had been hopefully converted a little before, at about eleven years of age, and then seriously talked to her about the great things of religion. Her parents did not know of it at that time, and were not wont, in the counsels they gave to their children, particularly to direct themselves to her, by reason of her being so young, and as they supposed, not capable of understanding. But after her brother had talked to her, they observed her very earnestly to listen to the advice they gave to the other children, and she was observed very constantly to retire several times in a day, as was concluded, for secret prayer, and grew more and more engaged in religion, and was more frequently in her closet, till at last she was wont to visit it five or six times in a day, and was so engaged in it that nothing would at any time divert her from her stated closet exercises. Her mother often observed and watched her when such things occurred, as she thought most likely to divert her, either by putting it out of her thoughts, or otherwise engaging her inclinations, but never could observe her to fail. She mentioned some very remarkable instances.

Phebe's Anxiety About the Hereafter

She once, of her own accord, spake of her unsuccessfulness, in that she could not find God, or to that purpose. But on Thursday, the last day of July, about the middle of the day, the child being in the closet, where it used to retire, its mother heard it speaking aloud, which was unusual and never had been observed before. And her voice seemed to be as of one exceeding importunate and engaged, but her mother could distinctly hear only these words (spoken in her childish manner, but seemed to be spoken with extraordinary earnestness, and out of

---

[1] Jonathan Edwards, "Narrative of Surprising Conversions," Works (New York: Leavitt, Trow & Co., 1844), Vol. III, pp. 265–267.

distress of soul), "Pray, blessed Lord, give me salvation! I pray, beg pardon all my sins!" When the child had done prayer she came out of the closet, and came and sat down by her mother, and cried out aloud. Her mother very earnestly asked her several times what the matter was, before she would make any answer. But she continued exceedingly crying and wreathing her body to and fro, like one in anguish of spirit. Her mother then asked her whether she was afraid that God would not give her salvation. She then answered, "Yes, I am afraid I shall go to hell!" Her mother then endeavored to quiet her, and told her she would not have her cry — she must be a good girl, and pray every day, and she hoped God would give her salvation. But this did not quiet her at all. But she continued thus earnestly crying and taking on for some time, till at length she suddenly ceased crying and began to smile, and presently said with a smiling countenance, "Mother, the kingdom of heaven is come to me!" Her mother was surprised at the sudden alteration and at the speech, and knew not what to make of it, but at first said nothing to her. The child presently spake again, and said, "There is another come to me, and there is another — there is three." And being asked what she meant, she answered, "One is, thy will be done, and there is another, enjoy him forever," by which it seems that when the child said, "There is three come to me," she meant three passages of its catechism that came to her mind.

Phebe Becomes Convinced of Her Salvation

After the child had said this, she retired again into her closet. And her mother went over to her brother's, who was next neighbor; and when she came back, the child being come out of the closet, meets her mother with this cheerful speech: "I can find God now!" Referring to what she had before complained of, that she could not find God. Then the child spoke again, and said: "I love God!" Her mother asked her how well she loved God, whether she loved God better than her father and mother. She said, "Yes." Then she asked her whether she loved God better than her little sister Rachel. She answered, "Yes, better than anything!" Then her eldest sister, referring to her saying she could find God now, asked her where she could find God. She answered, "In heaven." "Why," said she, "have you been in heaven?" "No," said the child. By this it seems not to have been any imagination of anything seen with bodily eyes that she called God, when she said, "I can find God now." Her mother asked her whether she was afraid of going to hell, and that had made her cry. She answered, "Yes, I was; but now I shall not." Her mother asked her whether she thought that God had given her salvation. She answered, "Yes." Her mother asked her when; she answered, "Today." She appeared all that afternoon exceeding cheerful and joyful. One of the neighbors asked her how she felt herself. She answered, "I feel better than I did." The neighbor asked her what made her feel better; she answered, "God makes me." That evening as she lay abed, she called one of her little cousins to her, that was present in the room, as having something to say to him; and when he came, she told him that heaven was better than earth. The next day being Friday, her mother asking her her catechism, asked her what God made her for. She answered, "To serve him," and added, "Everybody should serve God and get an interest in Christ."

The same day the older children, when they came home from school, seemed much affected with the extraordinary change that seemed to be made in Phebe; and her sister Abigail standing by, her mother took occasion to counsel her, now to improve her time to prepare for another world; on which Phebe burst out in tears, and cried out, "Poor Nabby!" Her mother told her she would not have her cry, she hoped that God would give Nabby salvation; but that did not quiet her, but she continued earnestly crying for some time. And when she had in a measure ceased, her sister Eunice being by her, she burst out again, and cried, "Poor Eunice!" And [she] cried exceedingly; and when she had almost done, she went into another room, and there looked upon her sister Naomi, and burst out again, crying, "Poor Amy!" Her mother was greatly affected at such a behavior in the child, and knew not what to say to her. One of the neighbors coming in a little after, asked her what she had cried for. She seemed at first backward to tell the reason. Her mother told her she might tell that person, for he had given her an apple, upon which she said she cried because she was afraid they would go to hell.

At night a certain minister that was occasionally in the town was at the house, and talked considerably with her of the things of religion. And after he was gone she sat leaning on the table with tears running out of her eyes; and being asked what made her cry she said it was thinking about God. The next day being Saturday, she seemed [for a] great part of the day to be in a very affectionate frame, had four turns of crying, and seemed to endeavor to curb herself and hide her tears, and was very backward to talk of the occasion of it. On the Sabbath day she was asked whether she believed in God; she answered, "Yes"; and being told that Christ was the Son of God, she made ready answer, and said, "I know it."

The Child's Devotion to Worship

From this time there has appeared a very remarkable abiding change in the child. She has been very strict upon the Sabbath, and seems to long for the Sabbath day before it comes, and will often in the week time be inquiring how long it is to the Sabbath day, and must have the days particularly counted over that are between, before she will be contented. And she seems to love God's house — is very eager to go thither. Her mother once asked her why she had such a mind to go, whether it was not to see fine folks. She said no, it was to hear Mr. Edwards preach. When she is in the place of worship, she is very far from spending her time there as children at her age usually do, but appears with an attention that is very extraordinary for such a child. She also appears very desirous at all opportunities to go to private religious meetings, and is very still and attentive at home in prayer time, and has appeared affected in time of family prayer. She seems to delight much in hearing religious conversation. When I once was there with some others that were strangers and talked to her something of religion, she seemed more than ordinarily attentive; and when we were gone, she looked out very wistfully after us, and said, "I wish they would come again!" Her mother asked her why. Says she, "I love to hear them talk!"

3. Recollections of Whitefield, the Revivalist[1]

✤ *Benjamin Franklin*

Benjamin Franklin, the genial spokesman for the Age of Reason, viewed George Whitefield's theology with no more than amiable tolerance; but Whitefield the man and revivalist interested him greatly. In his Autobiography, *Franklin gave a very fair picture of Whitefield and the effect his preaching had on*

[1] Benjamin Franklin, "Autobiography," in *Writings*, ed. A. H. Smyth (New York: The Macmillan Company, 1905), Vol. I, pp. 354–58.

multitudes. At the same time, his account suggests the wide divergence in religious attitudes between the evangelical and the rationalist halves of the eighteenth century. ■

In 1739 arrived among us from Ireland the Reverend Mr. Whitefield, who had made himself remarkable there as an itinerant preacher. He was at first permitted to preach in some of our churches; but the clergy, taking a dislike to him, soon refused him their pulpits, and he was obliged to preach in the fields. The multitudes of all sects and denominations that attended his sermons were enormous, and it was matter of speculation to me, who was one of the number, to observe the extraordinary influence of his oratory on his hearers, and how much they admired and respected him, notwithstanding his common abuse of them, by assuring them they were naturally half beasts and half devils. It was wonderful to see the change soon made in the manners of our inhabitants. From being thoughtless or indifferent about religion, it seemed as if all the world were growing religious, so that one could not walk through the town in an evening without hearing psalms sung in different families of every street. . . .

Whitefield's Project for an Orphanage in Georgia

I did not disapprove of the design, but, as Georgia was then destitute of materials and workmen, and it was proposed to send them from Philadelphia at a great expense, I thought it would have been better to have built the house here, and brought the children to it. This I advised; but he was resolute in his first project, rejected my counsel, and I therefore refused to contribute. I happened soon after to attend one of his sermons, in the course of which I perceived he intended to finish with a collection, and I silently resolved he should get nothing from me. I had in my pocket a handful of copper money, three or four silver dollars, and five pistoles [coins] in gold. As he proceeded I began to soften, and concluded to give the coppers. Another stroke of his oratory made me ashamed of that, and determined me to give the silver; and he finished so admirably, that I emptied my pocket wholly into the collector's dish, gold and all. At this sermon there was also one of our club, who, being of my sentiments respecting the building in Georgia, and suspecting a collection might be intended, had, by precaution, emptied his pockets before he came from home. Towards the conclusion of the discourse, however, he felt a strong desire to give, and applied to a neighbour, who stood near him to borrow some money for the purpose. The application was unfortunately [made] to perhaps the only man in the company who had the firmness not to be affected by the preacher. His answer was, "At any other time, Friend Hopkinson, I would lend to thee freely; but not now, for thee seems to be out of thy right senses."

A Civil Friendship

. . . He used sometimes to pray for my conversion, but never had the satisfaction of believing that his prayers were heard. Ours was a mere civil friendship, sincere on both sides, and lasted to his death.

The following instance will show something of the terms on which we stood. Upon one of his arrivals from England at Boston, he wrote to me that he should come soon to Philadelphia, but knew not where he could lodge when there, as he understood his old friend and host, Mr. Benezet was removed to Germantown. My answer was, "You know my house; if you can make shift with its scanty accommodations, you will be most heartily welcome." He replied that if I made that kind offer for Christ's sake, I should not miss of a reward. And I returned, "Don't let me be mistaken; it was not for Christ's sake, but for your sake." . . .

He had a loud and clear voice, and articulated his words and sentences so perfectly, that he might be heard and understood at a great distance, especially as his auditories, however numerous, observed the most exact silence. He preached one evening from the top of the Courthouse steps, which are in the middle of Market Street, and on the west side of Second Street, which crosses it at right angles. Both streets were filled with his hearers to a considerable distance. Being among the hindmost in Market Street, I had the curiosity to learn how far he could be heard, by retiring backwards down the street towards the river; and I found his voice distinct till I came near Front Street, when some noise in that street obscured it. Imagining then a semicircle, of which my distance should be the radius, and that it were filled with auditors, to each of whom I allowed two square feet, I computed that he might well be heard by more than thirty thousand. This reconciled me to the newspaper accounts of his having preached to twenty-five thousand people in the fields, and to the ancient histories of generals haranguing whole armies, of which I had sometimes doubted.

4. Religious Liberalism Emerges[1]

✤ John Bass

In Christian theology, one of the questions repeatedly discussed is the relationship between a man's deeds in this life and his eternal salvation. In Protestant theology, Calvinism — named for the French theologian John Calvin (1509–1564) — argues that salvation is wholly an unmerited gift from God. On the other hand, Arminianism — named for the Dutch theologian Jacobus Arminius (1560–1609) — replies that God's decree with respect to the salvation of a man is a conditional one, dependent on his own act of belief and repentance. While Arminianism is not inconsistent with revivalism, in those traditions where revivalism and Calvinism were identified with one another, the reaction against revivalism often led to a reaction against Calvinism also. The personal narrative of John Bass, of Ashford, Connecticut, soon after the Great Awakening, suggests how this might take place. ∎

When I was settled in the ministry at Ashford, which was in the year 1743, I was, and professed myself to be, of the *Calvinian* class; and as such I remained for several years; yet all that time suspected by some of my very zealous and critical hearers; and was accordingly harassed by them, charged with Arminianism and what not, accused before counsels and pelted with insults. Yet so long as I remained orthodox I stood my ground, and always came off with victory. But, alas, alas! when this failed, though my adversaries will not say I wanted anything else, I fell. Calvinistic principles I then found to be at this day a clergyman's main defence; the best he can hit upon to provide him food and raiment, and to fix him in the good graces of the populace: interest set this way. Nevertheless so imprudent was I, that to please my conscience, I must examine anew the foundation of my faith, the truth of those principles I had professed and preached for years before. And the effect of this was, I found myself obliged to recant some former sentiments; and, as you will see by and by, to

[1] John Bass, *A True Narrative of an Unhappy Contention in the Church at Ashford*. Boston: D. Gookin, 1751), pp. 3–5, 23.

come into a new and different scheme, or set of notions.[2] Then I must leave out of my public performances those notions which were peculiar to Calvinism, which being discovered by some of my eagle-eyed people, their jealousy revived and grew stronger than ever; and though for a time this was but whispered among them, at length it broke out in a flaming contention, which has unhappily issued in such a breach, not only betwixt the greater part of the people and myself; but also betwixt the people themselves, as 'tis highly probable will never be healed.

'Twas some time in December last [1750], that I entertained my people with a public discourse from those words of St. Paul, in I Thes. 5.21: *Prove all things; hold fast that which is good.* At which discourse, though I meddled with no controversial point, yet as I advised them to a careful, unprejudiced enquiry after the will of God as revealed in the Bible, and not to content themselves with a religion at second-hand, they were some of them extremely displeased, supposing (I conclude) such advice had no favorable aspect upon their particular notions. Now it was that some were too uneasy to sit still any longer; and as the administration of the Supper was to be on the next Sabbath, something they thought must be immediately done — they itched, it seemed, to have me in their clutches, but how to attack me they were at a loss. I had not, as yet, spoken out my sentiments upon the controverted points hereafter mentioned, except to a friend in the corners. But as two brethren of the Church of Christ who were known to be my friends had, it was resolved to fall upon them in the first place. Being strongly importuned by some of the dissatisfied, I went with them to converse with those two brethren; and though I did not then, as I remember, declare my own sentiments upon the points in dispute, but, to excite them to mutual charity and forbearance, endeavored to let them see that much could be said on both sides, they apparently became more confirmed in their suspicion of me than before. And to such a surprising length did some carry their groundless resentment, that on the next Lord's Day they withdrew from the ordinance of the Supper, thereby proclaiming abroad their discontent, which spread among the people as they became acquainted with the grounds of it. There was presently a general commotion among them; and within a few days after, a detachment

---

[2] These I did not in my sermons publish to my people; because I thought they could not bear them as yet. [Bass's note.]

from the aggrieved came to my house, and requested a church meeting. My answer was that as the people were generally in a ruffle, 'twas in my opinion best to defer calling them together till they were cooler and so fitter for action. This was not at all pleasing to them; and all I could say was to little effect. . . .

Bass Is Dismissed by a Council

It now [appears] to this council that the most of this church are dissatisfied and aggrieved with the principles of their pastor the Rev'd Mr. John Bass and complaining that he has departed from those principles he professed and declared in the confession of faith which he subscribed when he settled here, and declared to be his leading principles, which he was resolved by the grace of Christ to maintain and inculcate, and that most of the church remain firm in the belief of those principles: [they] therefore desire the said Mr. Bass may be dismissed and removed from them.

This council finds that the sentiments and principles of the Rev. Mr. Bass (as he himself has expressed and declared them in the said paper delivered in to us) are now very different from what they were as contained in the aforesaid confession of faith; and we think that this difference (which we apprehend to be a departure from the true doctrine of the Gospel, and also from the principles to [which] the generality of the church do adhere) is sufficient ground for the dissolution of the pastoral relation of the said Mr. Bass to this church; and [we] do according to the desire of the church declare the pastoral relation of Mr. Bass to this church to be dissolved, and [declare] that he is dismissed from this church and people.

5. Methodist Revivalism in Virginia[1]

✤ *Devereux Jarratt*

In Virginia, the foremost spokesman for evangelical religion in the latter part of the eighteenth century was the Reverend Devereux Jarratt (1733–1801). Unlike most of his fellow min-

[1] Devereux Jarratt, "A Brief Narrative of the Revival of Religion in Virginia," in Francis Asbury, *Journal and Letters*, ed. E. T. Clark (Nashville: Abingdon Press, 1958), Vol. I, pp. 207–208, 209–210, 212.

*isters of the Church of England, who were rationalistic in temper,
Jarratt preached a gospel of conversion, and co-operated with
Methodist missionaries. Though he himself did not join
Methodism when it separated from the Anglican church to be-
come a distinct denomination, he contributed much to its early
growth in Virginia.* ■

DEAR SIR, You were pleased, when in Virginia, to desire a narrative
of the work of God in these parts. I shall give you matter of fact, in a
plain, artless dress; relating only what I have myself seen and heard,
and what I have received from men on whose judgment and veracity
I can fully depend.

That you may have a full view of the whole, I shall go back as far
as my first settlement in this parish. August 29, 1763, I was chosen
rector of Bath, in the county of Dinwiddie, in Virginia. Ignorance of
the things of God, profaneness, and irreligion, then prevailed among
all ranks and degrees. So that I doubt if even the form of godliness
was to be found in any one family of this large and populous parish.
I was a stranger to the people: my doctrines were quite new to them;
and were neither preached nor believed by any other clergyman, so
far as I could learn, throughout the province.

My first work was to explain the depravity of our nature; our fall in
Adam, and all the evils consequent thereon; the impossibility of being
delivered from them by anything which we could do; and the necessity
of a living faith, in order to our obtaining help from God. While I
continued to insist upon these truths, and on the absolute necessity
of being born again, no small outcry was raised against this way, as
well as against him that taught it. But by the help of God, I continued to witness the same both to small and great.

The common people, however, frequented the church more constantly, and in larger numbers than usual. Some were affected at
times, so as to drop a tear. But still, for a year or more, I perceived
no lasting effect, only a few were not altogether so profane as before.
I could discover no heartfelt convictions of sin, no deep or lasting
impression of their lost estate. Indeed I have reason to believe that
some have been a good deal alarmed at times. But they were shy of
speaking to me (thinking it would be presumption) till their convictions wore off.

But in the year 1765, the power of God was more sensibly felt by a few. These were constrained to apply to me, and inquire what they must do to be saved. And now I began to preach abroad, as well as in private houses; and to meet little companies in the evenings, and converse freely on divine things. I believe some were this year converted to God, and thenceforth the work of God slowly went on. . . .

Co-operation with Methodist Itinerant Preachers

I earnestly recommended it to my societies to pray much for the prosperity of Zion, and for a larger outpouring of the Spirit of God. They did so; and not in vain. We have had a time of refreshing indeed: a revival of religion, as great as perhaps ever was known in country places in so short a time. It began in the latter end of the year 1775, but was more considerable in January, 1776, the beginning of the present year. It broke out nearly at the same time, at three places not far from each other. Two of these places are in my parish, the other in Amelia county — which had for many years been notorious for carelessness, profaneness, and immoralities of all kinds. Gaming, swearing, drunkenness, and the like, were their delight, while things sacred were their scorn and contempt. However, some time last year one of my parish (now a local preacher) appointed some meetings among them, and after a while induced a small number to join in society. And though few, if any of them were then believers, yet this was a means of preparing the way of the Lord.

As there were few converts in my parish the last year, I was sensible a change of preachers was wanting. This has often revived the work of God, and so it did at the present time. Last December one of the Methodist preachers, Mr. Shadford, preached several times at the three places abovementioned. He confirmed the doctrine I had long preached, and to many of them not in vain. And while their ears were opened by novelty, God set his word home upon their hearts. Many sinners were powerfully convinced, and "Mercy! mercy!" was their cry. In January, the news of convictions and conversions was common; and the people of God were inspired with new life and vigor by the happiness of others. But in a little time they were made thoroughly sensible that they themselves stood in need of a deeper work in their hearts than they had yet experienced. And while those were panting and groaning for pardon, these were entreating God, with strong cries and tears, to save them from the remains of inbred sin, to "sanctify them throughout, in spirit, soul, and body;" so to "circumcise their hearts," that they might "love God with all their hearts," and serve him with all their strength.

During this whole winter, the Spirit of the Lord was poured out in a manner we had not seen before. In almost every assembly might be seen signal instances of divine power, more especially in the meeting of the classes. Here many old stout-hearted sinners felt the force of truth, and their eyes were open to discover their guilt and danger. The shaking among the dry bones was increased from week to week; nay, sometimes ten or twelve have been deeply convinced of sin in one day. Some of these were in great distress, and when they were questioned concerning the state of their souls, were scarce able to make any reply but by weeping and falling on their knees before all the class, and earnestly soliciting the prayers of God's people. And from time to time he has answered these petitions, set the captives at liberty, and enabled them to praise a pardoning God in the midst of his people. Numbers of old and gray-headed, of middle-aged persons, of youth, yea, of little children, were the subjects of this work. Several of the latter we have seen painfully concerned for the wickedness of their lives and the corruption of their nature. We have instances of this sort from eight or nine years old. Some of these children are exceeding happy in the love of God — and they speak of the whole process of the work of God, of their convictions, the time when, and the manner how, they obtained deliverance — with such clearness as might convince an atheist that this is nothing else but the great power of God.

Many in these parts who had long neglected the means of grace now flocked to hear, not only me and the travelling preachers, but also the exhorters and leaders. And the Lord showed he is not confined to man; for whether there was preaching or not, his power was still sensible among the people. And at their meetings for prayer, some have been in such distress that they have continued therein for five or six hours. And it has been found that these prayer meetings were singularly useful in promoting the work of God.

The outpouring of the Spirit which began here soon extended itself, more or less, through most of the circuit, which is regularly attended by the travelling preachers, and which takes in a circumference of between four and five hundred miles. . . .

It has been frequently observed, that there never was any remarkable revival of religion, but some degree of enthusiasm was mingled with it — some wildfire mixed with the sacred flame. It may be doubted whether this is not unavoidable in the nature of things. And notwithstanding all the care we have taken, this work has not been quite free from it; but it never rose to any considerable height, neither was of long continuance. In some meetings there has not been that decency and order observed which I could have wished. Some of our assemblies resembled the congregation of the Jews at laying the foundation of the second temple in the days of Ezra — some wept for grief; others shouted for joy; so that it was hard to distinguish one from the other. So it was here: the mourning and distress were so blended with the voice of joy and gladness, that it was hard to distinguish the one from the other, till the voice of joy prevailed — the people shouting with a great shout, so that it might be heard afar off.

IV. Revolutionary Times

The American Revolution brought about changes in ecclesiastical institutions as well as political ones. Thus the Church of England had to reorganize as the Protestant Episcopal Church in the United States of America; and the Presbyterians at the same time were developing a national organization. But in addition, the Revolution gave impetus to the movement for separation of church and state, for which religious minorities were already agitating. The political theory of the Revolution declared that governments are organized for the protection of life, liberty, and property in this world. Religion, so the argument went, has to do with a man's obligations toward his Creator, and his preparation for the world to come. Governments therefore have no business supporting or giving direct encouragement to churches, since their concerns lie outside the proper sphere of political government. The logic seemed simple and straightforward to men like Thomas Jefferson. But not everyone was persuaded by it then, or accepts it now. ■

1. Religious Freedom in Virginia[1]

✢ Thomas Jefferson

Thomas Jefferson was not an irreligious man, though his political opponents tried to persuade the voters that he was. But he adhered to a very private concept of religion, and considered a man's religious beliefs to be his own business and no one else's. Since he lacked a sense of religion as an expression of corporate or group experience, it was axiomatic for him that it should be left for the individual to deal with as he saw fit; and that government should accordingly not interfere, either to suppress heresy or support orthodoxy. The "Notes on Virginia,"

[1] Thomas Jefferson, "Notes on Virginia," in *Writings*, Definitive Edition (Washington, D.C.: Thomas Jefferson Memorial Association, 1905), Vol. II, pp. 221–24.

from which this selection is taken, was written in 1781–83. The policy Jefferson advocated found expression in the Virginia Statute of Religious Freedom (1785), of which Jefferson was the author. ∎

. . . The error seems not sufficiently eradicated, that the operations of the mind, as well as the acts of the body, are subject to the coercion of the laws. But our rulers can have no authority over such natural rights, only as we have submitted to them. The rights of conscience we never submitted, we could not submit. We are answerable for them to our God. The legitimate powers of government extend to such acts only as are injurious to others. But it does me no injury for my neighbor to say there are twenty gods, or no God. It neither picks my pocket nor breaks my leg. If it be said, his testimony in a court of justice cannot be relied on, reject it then, and be the stigma on him. Constraint may make him worse by making him a hypocrite, but it will never make him a truer man. It may fix him obstinately in his errors, but will not cure them.

Reason and free inquiry are the only effectual agents against error. Give a loose to them, they will support the true religion by bringing every false one to their tribunal, to the test of their investigation. They are the natural enemies of error, and of error only. Had not the Roman government permitted free inquiry, Christianity could never have been introduced. Had not free inquiry been indulged at the era of the Reformation, the corruptions of Christianity could not have been purged away. If it be restrained now, the present corruptions will be protected and new ones encouraged. Was the government to prescribe to us our medicine and diet, our bodies would be in such keeping as our souls are now. Thus in France the emetic was once forbidden as a medicine, and the potato as an article of food. Government is just as infallible, too, when it fixes systems in physics. Galileo was sent to the Inquisition for affirming that the earth was a sphere; the government had declared it to be as flat as a trencher, and Galileo was obliged to abjure his error. This error, however, at length prevailed, the earth became a globe, and Descartes declared it was whirled round its axis by a vortex. The government in which he lived was wise enough to see that this was no question of civil jurisdiction, or we should all have been involved by authority

in vortices. In fact, the vortices have been exploded, and the New-
tonian principle of gravitation is now more firmly established on the
basis of reason than it would be were the government to step in and
to make it an article of necessary faith. Reason and experiment have
been indulged, and error has fled before them.

It is error alone which needs the support of government. Truth can
stand by itself. Subject opinion to coercion — whom will you make
your inquisitors? Fallible men — men governed by bad passions, by
private as well as public reasons. And why subject it to coercion? To
produce uniformity. But is uniformity of opinion desirable? No
more than of face and stature. Introduce the bed of Procrustes[2] then,
and as there is danger that the large men may beat the small, make us
all of a size by lopping the former and stretching the latter. Difference of opinion is advantageous in religion. The several sects perform the office of a *censor morum*[3] over such other. Is uniformity
attainable? Millions of innocent men, women, and children, since
the introduction of Christianity, have been burnt, tortured, fined,
imprisoned; yet we have not advanced one inch towards uniformity.
What has been the effect of coercion? To make one half the world
fools, and the other half hypocrites. To support roguery and error
all over the earth. Let us reflect that it is inhabited by a thousand
millions of people. That these profess probably a thousand different
systems of religion. That ours is but one of that thousand. That if
there be but one right, and ours that one, we should wish to see the
nine hundred and ninety-nine wandering sects gathered into the fold
of truth. But against such a majority we cannot effect this by force.
Reason and persuasion are the only practicable instruments.

To make way for these, free inquiry must be indulged. And how
can we wish others to indulge it while we refuse it ourselves? But
every state, says an inquisitor, has established some religion. No two,
say I, have established the same. Is this a proof of the infallibility of
establishments? Our sister states of Pennsylvania and New York,
however, have long subsisted without any establishment at all. The
experiment was new and doubtful when they made it. It has an-

[2] [bed of Procrustes: an arbitrary standard to which exact conformity is demanded. Procrustes was a legendary Greek giant who stretched or shortened his
captives to fit one of his iron beds.]

[3] [censor morum: censor (or supervisor) of public morality (Latin).]

HISTORIC HOUSES OF WORSHIP: *Religious edifices are an important part of the American spiritual heritage. For the most part they were modest structures, reflecting the humble circumstances of the worshipers. The Friends Meeting House, Flushing, New York (right), was built in 1694 and is one of the oldest houses of worship in the United States. Its unadorned simplicity is characteristic of the unassuming faith of the early Quakers.*

The Old Methodist Church of New York (left), completed in 1768, was the first church of that denomination built in America. The Old Rehoboth Methodist Church in Monroe County, West Virginia, was built in 1786. It is the oldest Protestant church west of the Alleghenies. The roughhewn log church became a familiar sight along the western frontier.

The Mission Dolores (right), built in 1776, was the first church in San Francisco. It was one of many Spanish missions built along the Pacific Coast and predated the arrival of English-speaking settlers in California.

The Temple Jeshuat Israel (left) of Touro Street, Newport, Rhode Island, is probably the oldest synagogue in America. Jews first settled Newport in 1658 and built the synagogue in 1763. Newport remained an important Jewish community throughout the colonial period.

The Old Russian Chapel (right) of Fort Ross, California, is one of the oldest Eastern Orthodox churches in the United States. It was built in 1812 by a company of Russian fur-traders. The Eastern Orthodox faith was introduced into America by Russian traders and settlers in Alaska and along the Pacific coastline.

swered beyond conception. They flourish infinitely. Religion is well supported; of various kinds, indeed, but all good enough; all sufficient to preserve peace and order; or if a sect arises whose tenets would subvert morals, good sense has fair play and reasons and laughs it out of doors without suffering the state to be troubled with it. They do not hang more malefactors than we do. They are not more disturbed with religious dissensions. On the contrary, their harmony is unparalleled, and can be ascribed to nothing but their unbounded tolerance, because there is no other circumstance in which they differ from every nation on earth. They have made the happy discovery that the way to silence religious disputes is to take no notice of them. Let us too give this experiment fair play, and get rid, while we may, of those tyrannical laws. . . .

2. Public Support of Religion in Massachusetts[1]

✤ *Theophilus Parsons*

Because Americans generally accept a policy of separation of church and state — though they still cannot agree in all particulars as to what this means — it does not follow that they have accepted Jefferson's assumption that religion is a private affair, of concern to the individual rather than society at large. Americans have more often supposed that government rests on a moral consensus, and morality can never be wholly disentangled from religion; hence religious values whether in familiar or disguised form are involved in the survival of secular government itself. That is the basic argument for patronage of religion by the state; and it is found in classic form in Theophilus Parson's defense of the tax support of religion in Massachusetts, presented here.

Experience showed, however, that the kind of public support of religious institutions that Parsons thought essential to civil society was unacceptable in a religiously pluralistic community. Americans since the early nineteenth century have tended to agree with Parsons that society depends on a consensus as to basic values rooted in religion, while rejecting his conclusion that this consensus is fostered by public support of the churches ■

[1] Parsons, C. J., *Barnes v. First Parish in Falmouth*, 6 Mass. 401 (1810).

The object of a free civil government is the promotion and security of the happiness of the citizens. These effects cannot be produced, but by the knowledge and practice of our moral duties, which comprehend all the social and civil obligations of man to man, and of the citizen to the state. If the civil magistrate in any state could procure by his regulations a uniform practice of these duties, the government of that state would be perfect.

To obtain that perfection it is not enough for the magistrate to define the rights of the several citizens as they are related to life, liberty, property, and reputation, and to punish those by whom they may be invaded. . . . Human laws cannot oblige to the performance of the duties of imperfect obligation; as the duties of charity and hospitality, benevolence and good neighborhood; as the duties resulting from the relation of husband and wife, parent and child; of man to man, as children of a common parent; and of real patriotism, by influencing every citizen to love his country, and to obey all its laws. These are moral duties, flowing from the disposition of the heart, and not subject to the control of human legislation. . . .

Civil government, therefore, availing itself only of its own powers, is extremely defective; and unless it could derive assistance from some superior power, whose laws extend to the temper and disposition of the human heart, and before whom no offence is secret, wretched indeed would be the state of man under a civil constitution of any form. . . .

Tax Support of Protestant Christianity in Massachusetts

On these principles, tested by the experience of mankind and by the reflections of reason, the people of Massachusetts, in the frame of their government, adopted and patronized a religion, which, by its benign and energetic influences, might co-operate with human institutions to promote and secure the happiness of the citizens, so far as might be consistent with the imperfections of man.

. . . This religion was found to rest on the basis of immortal truth; to contain a system of morals adapted to man in all possible ranks and conditions, situations and circumstances, by conforming to which he would be meliorated and improved in all the relations of human life; and to furnish the most efficacious sanctions by bringing to light a future state of retribution. And this religion, as understood by Protestants, tending, by its effects, to make every man submitting to its influence a better husband, parent, child, neighbor, citizen, and magistrate, was by the people established as a fundamental and essential part of their constitution.

An Objection Answered

The second objection is that it is intolerant to compel a man to pay for religious instruction from which, as he does not hear it, he can derive no benefit. This objection is founded wholly in mistake. The object of public religious instruction is to teach, and to enforce by suitable arguments the practice of a system of correct morals among the people, and to form and cultivate reasonable and just habits and manners, by which every man's person and property are protected from outrage and his personal and social enjoyments promoted and multiplied. From these effects every man derives the most important benefits; and whether he be, or be not, an auditor of any public teacher, he receives more solid and permanent advantages from this public instruction than the administration of justice in courts of law can give him. The like objection may be made by any man to the support of public schools if he have no family who attend; and any man who has no lawsuit may object to the support of judges and jurors on the same ground, when, if there were no courts of law, he would unfortunately find that causes for lawsuits would sufficiently abound.

3. The Americanization of the Church of England[1]
♣ William White

The American Revolution put the Church of England in this country in a most awkward position. In the northern colonies, it was identified with the loyalist cause. In Virginia and other southern colonies, it had been the established church; but now the revolutionary tide was running against establishments of reli-

[1] William White, *The Case of the Episcopal Churches in the United States Considered* (Philadelphia, 1782; reprinted Philadelphia: J. Hamilton, 1859), pp. 3–6.

To form an idea of the situation of the Episcopal churches in the present crisis we must observe the change their religious system has undergone in the late revolution. . . .

It may reasonably be presumed that, in general, the members of the Episcopal churches are friendly to the principles on which the present governments were formed; a fact particularly obvious in the southern states, where the Episcopalians, who are a majority of the citizens, have engaged and persevered in the war with as much ardor and constancy as their neighbors. Many even of those whose sentiments were at first unfavorable to the revolution now wish for its final establishment as a most happy event, some from an earnest desire of peace, and others from the undistinguishing oppressions and ravages of the British armies. Such persons accordingly acknowledge allegiance and pay obedience to the sovereignty of the states.

Inconsistent with the duties resulting from this allegiance would be their subjection to any spiritual jurisdiction connected with the temporal authority of a foreign state. Such a dependence is contrary to the fundamental principles of civil society, and therefore cannot be required by the Scriptures; which, being accommodated to the civil policy of the world at large, neither interfered with the constitution of states as found established at the time of their promulgation, nor handed down to succeeding ages any injunction of such a tendency.

To apply these observations to the case of the Episcopal churches in the United States. They have heretofore been subject to the ecclesiastical authority of the bishop of London. This authority was derived under a commission from the Crown; which, though destitute of legal operation, found a general acquiescence on the part of the churches being exercised no farther than to the necessary purposes of ordaining and licensing ministers. Hereby a connection was formed between the spiritual authority in England and the Episcopal churches in America, the latter constituting a part of the bishop of London's diocese.

But this connection is dissolved by the [American] Revolution. . . . Even suppose the bishop of London hereafter exempted, by act of Parliament, from the necessity of exacting the oaths,[2] a dependence on his Lordship and his successors in that see would be liable to the reproach of foreign influence, and render Episcopalians less qualified than those of other communions to be trusted by their country. . . .

The ecclesiastical power over the greater number of the churches, formerly subsisting in some legislative bodies on this continent, is also abrogated by the revolution. In the southern states, where the Episcopal churches were maintained by law, the assemblies might well have been supposed empowered, in conjunction with the other branches of legislation, to regulate their external government; but now, when the establishments are overturned, it would ill become those bodies, composed of men of various denominations (however respectable collectively and as individuals), to enact laws for the Episcopal churches, which will no doubt, in common with others, claim and exercise the privilege of governing themselves.

All former jurisdiction over the churches being thus withdrawn, and the chain which held them together broken, it would seem that their future continuance can be provided for only by voluntary associations for union and good government.

A Democratized Version of Episcopal Government

The power of electing a superior order of ministers ought to be in the clergy and laity together, they being both interested in the choice. In England, the bishops are appointed by the civil authority, which was an usurpation of the Crown at the Norman conquest, but since confirmed by acts of Parliament. The primitive churches were generally supplied by popular elections; even in the city of Rome, the privilege of electing the bishops continued with the people till the tenth or eleventh century; and near those times there are resolves of councils that none shall be promoted to ecclesiastical dignities but by the election of the clergy and people. It cannot be denied that this

---

[2] [oaths: the oaths of allegiance to the king of England as head of the Church of England, required of the clergy of that church.]

right vested in numerous bodies occasioned great disorders, which it is expected will be avoided when the people shall exercise the right of representation.

In England dioceses have been formed before parishes. A church supposes one common flock, subject to a bishop and sundry collegiate presbyters, without the idea of its being necessarily divided into smaller communities connected with their respective parochial clergy, the latter having been introduced some time after the conversion of the nation to the Christian faith. One natural consequence of this distinction will be to retain in each church every power that need not be delegated for the good of the whole. Another will be an equality of the churches, and not, as in England, the subjection of all parish churches to their respective cathedrals.

4. Roman Catholicism and American Pluralism[1]

✠ *John Carroll*

The Roman Catholics, like the Episcopalians, were compelled by the Revolution to reorganize their ecclesiastical structure so as to eliminate English supervision or control. Dr. John Carroll, born in Maryland in 1735, was the outstanding American Catholic churchman; and in 1790, he became the first Bishop of Baltimore, as the explicit choice of the American clergy. Following his consecration, he published a pamphlet in which the sermon delivered on that occasion was prefaced by a brief history of Catholicism in America. Recalling the persecution they had encountered in colonial America, Catholics like Carroll welcomed the enlarging spirit of religious freedom as appropriate for a pluralistic society. ∎

The Roman Catholic religion was introduced into Maryland, together with the first settlers in the reign of Charles I, who granted that province to the Lord Baltimore, a Catholic nobleman, as a refuge for persons of his religion from the severity of the penal laws which that unfortunate monarch wanted either the power or the fortitude to

---

[1] [John Carroll], *A Short Account of the Establishment of the New See of Baltimore, Maryland* (Philadelphia: Carey, Stewart & Co., 1791), pp. 1–4.

restrain. A number of Catholic gentlemen and others emigrated from England and Ireland with the hope of enjoying that repose in the new settlement which was denied them in their native country. The unrelenting spirit of persecution pursued them over the Atlantic. It deprived them of the just fruits of their labors; it debarred them from every post of trust and profit in the colony which they had settled; it compelled them to maintain Protestant ministers, and finally, it enforced against them many of the British penal laws, from the cruelty of which they had fled. Reverend Father Andrew White, an English Jesuit of eminent piety and zeal, accompanied the first colonists in 1632, and from that date till the late Revolution the American Catholics in Maryland and Virginia were constantly served by Jesuit missioners successively sent from England. About the year 1720 the Reverend Father Grayton and others introduced Catholicity into Pennsylvania, and it has since received a remarkable increase in that province. Since the peace of 1783 and the settlement of the American Constitution, penal laws are no longer known, and Catholics enjoy an equal participation of the rights of human nature with their neighbors of every other religious denomination. The very term of *toleration* is exploded, because it imports a power in one predominant sect to indulge that religious liberty to others, which all claim as an inherent right. Catholic clergymen of various orders and nations have resorted to America, and they everywhere find an ample vineyard to cultivate. In this state of religious freedom the clergymen judged it expedient to give stability and dignity to the Catholic religion by the establishment of a regular hierarchy, and they therefore petitioned from the Pope the creation of an episcopal see and the appointment of a diocesan bishop. The Pope, applauding their zeal, graciously admitted their request and allowed them to elect their first bishop. The Rev. Dr. John Carroll, who had been for some years the superior of the mission, was the object of their choice, and this gentleman was accordingly appointed first bishop of Baltimore. Upon the receipt of his bulls[2] from Rome he immediately repaired to England where his person and merit were well known, and presented himself for consecration to the Right Rev. Dr. Charles Walmesley, Bishop of Rama, senior Vicar Apostolical of the Catholic religion in this kingdom. By invitation of Thomas Weld, Esq., the consecration of the new Bishop

---

[2] [**bulls:** official documents or credentials affixed with the Papal seal (bulla).]

was performed during a solemn high Mass in the elegant chapel at Lulworth Castle[3] on Sunday, the 15th day of August, 1790, being the feast of the Assumption of the Blessed Virgin Mary, and the munificence of that gentleman omitted no circumstance which could possibly add dignity to so venerable a ceremony. The two prelates were attended by their respective assistant priests and acolytes according to the rubric of the Roman Pontifical; the richness of their vestments, the music of the choir, the multitude of wax lights, and the ornaments of the altar concurred to increase the splendor of the solemnity, which made a lasting impression upon every beholder.

[3] [**Lulworth Castle:** near the village of Lulworth, in the county of Dorset, near the south coast of England.]

5. An Italian Visitor's Impressions[1]
✤ Giovanni Grassi

By the beginning of the nineteenth century, religious life in the United States had assumed a form that in many respects seems familiar to us today. If one did not realize that the following description was based on impressions received in the period 1810 to 1817, one would be hard put to say precisely what the date of it was. Here we find religious pluralism, accompanied by official toleration of all religious groups, and, at the same time, strong public opinion in favor of religious values in general. ■

Nothing is more striking to the Italian at his arrival in America than the state of religion. By virtue of an article in the federal constitution every religion and every sect is fully tolerated, is equally protected, and equally treated in the United States, at least if its principles or practices do not disturb the civil order and established law. Or, to put it more precisely, the government will not interfere in purely religious matters.

The number of those who openly deny the revelations is not as large as might be supposed, considering that this country is the refuge

[1] Oscar Handlin, ed., *This Was America* (Cambridge: Harvard University Press, 1949), pp. 147–150.

of all sorts of European wretches. The bulk of atheists is restricted to the French, who abandon the religion of their ancestors but rarely assume a non-Catholic belief.

Indifference, which is so common in the Europe of our times, takes on a special character in America. It does not consist of despising and giving up all practice of religion; many people continue to speak of religion and, generally, with respect. What then? They act as if God had never manifested his will to men, never pointed out the narrow path to salvation that is followed by a few, had never warned that there are other, broader, easier ones traveled by many whose principles seem correct but which ultimately lead to inevitable perdition — in a word, as if the Bible, so highly esteemed, so often read, and seized by all as rule of their religion, does not speak of an infallible God. Every sect there is held as good, every road as correct, and every error as the insignificant weakness of poor mortals.

In accordance with such principles, it is not surprising if America gives birth to innumerable sects which daily subdivide and multiply. Although how can one speak of sects? Those who describe themselves as members of one or another of the sects do not thereby profess an abiding adherence to the doctrines of the founders of the sect; they simply call themselves by the name of the sect to express the fact that they are not without any religion and that they frequent assemblies of a certain kind, or that they are brought up within a certain persuasion, whatever may be the actual state of their thoughts. Thus the Anglicans of today no longer take much account of their thirty-nine articles, nor the Lutherans of the Confession of Augsburg, nor the Presbyterians of the teachings of Calvin or of Knox. On the contrary, imitating the example of their masters, they examine, change, and decide as seems best at the time.

The very word *sect* does not have in America the derogatory meaning that etymology and usage have given it among us, so that a man there does not have the slightest hesitation in saying, "I belong to such a sect." Among the peculiarities of America, not the most extreme is that of finding persons who live together for several years without knowing each other's religion. And many, when asked, do not answer, "I believe," but simply, "I was brought up in such a persuasion."

Better to explain how religion is regarded here, I will give a few examples. In Georgetown, a suburb of Washington, there was a militia regiment which was, in accordance with its regulations, obliged to go to church each Sunday. But since the members belonged to various sects it was not easy to decide to which church or meeting to go. The matter was diplomatically adjusted as follows: they would go one Sunday to the Catholic church, another to the Methodist, a third to the Anglican, then to the Calvinist, and so on until they completed the circle, when they would start over again. . . .

Despite the indifference as to sect, there is, especially in the North, much show of piety. Everyone reads the Bible, and in New England they will not permit a traveler or allow a messenger to continue his journey on a Sunday. Also, almost every year petitions are presented to Congress to prohibit by law journeys on the Lord's Day. The captain of the ship on which I sailed from America to Europe would not allow the passengers to play dominoes or to sing on Sunday. Yet when we arrived in port of a Sunday morning he made the sailors work the whole day without the slightest reason. The observation of holidays in the North was formerly carried out to truly extravagant rigor. In certain states religious laws still remain on the statute book, particularly those which insist on the observation of the third commandment. These laws, although not repealed, are no longer rigorously enforced, and are called the Blue Laws.

From the arbitrary interpretation of the holy scriptures come results often truly lamentable. People with the best of wills are agitated by all the winds of doctrine. In Southington, Connecticut, there are some who read in the Bible that God commands the sanctification of the Sabbath; they observe precisely the Sabbath and not Sunday. There is a sect in Pennsylvania called the Harmony Society, which is directed by a chief who explains the Bible to them. Several years ago, having found in Saint Paul that virginity is better than matrimony, he promulgated an ordinance that all should observe chastity. There were sharp remonstrances that *melius est nubere quam uri*,[2] but all was in vain; the leader was inflexible. In Virginia, in the spring of 1812, a preacher announced from his pulpit the fatal prediction that on the fourth of July of that year would come the end of the world. The people believed it true, and let the season go by without planting or cultivating their fields, saying, why should they trouble to work since the end of the world would surely come before the harvest.

[2] [melius est nubere quam uri: "it is better to marry than to burn" I Cor. 7.9, as found in the King James Version.]

. *Part Two*

American Religion and American Destiny

Part Two: Introduction

From the colonial period of their history, Americans inherited a pattern of religious pluralism, which made inevitable a policy of neutrality on the part of the state toward competing religious groups, and voluntary support of religion by the members of each sect or denomination. Public opinion was friendly to religion, however, and America's destiny was commonly stated in language the imagery of which was drawn from the Bible. God's "almost chosen people" — the phrase is Lincoln's — were still considered to be under his providential care, entrusted with a civilizing mission for the whole world, and moving steadily toward a universal reign of righteousness and peace.

This cluster of ideas was especially characteristic of the evangelical Protestant churches. Central to evangelical Protestantism is the assertion that sinful men need to have an experience of conversion if they are to be saved. Its spokesmen therefore encouraged revivalism, and they organized voluntary societies for the promotion of benevolent causes, such as home and foreign missions, temperance reform, and antislavery. In this way, they believed, Americans would find the path to salvation and the nation's millennial hopes would be fulfilled. ■

V. Evangelical Protestantism

The term "evangelical Protestantism" does not refer to any single religious denomination. Many denominations were either predominantly evangelical, or had a strongly evangelical wing. Evangelicals of different denominations often co-operated in revivalistic activity, and in home and foreign missionary work. Hence, despite denominational distinctions, the dominant tone of American religion in the early nineteenth century was evangelical. Even dissenting religious groups often understood themselves in terms of the extent to which they disagreed with the evangelical position. ■

1. The Cane Ridge Camp Meeting[1]
✤ Barton W. Stone

After the Great Awakening, a continuous revivalistic tradition in America may be discerned. In the nineteenth century, however, revivalism assumed new forms and adopted new methods. On the western frontier, there developed the camp meeting, which brought people together from far and near for several days of religious services, preaching, and prayer. One of the first of these was in 1801, at Cane Ridge, Kentucky. The description that follows is from the autobiography of Barton W. Stone, who at the time was a Presbyterian minister nearby. Later he became associated with Alexander Campbell as a leader of the Christian Church (at various times and places known as Disciples of Christ or Churches of Christ). ■

We hurried up from Muhlenberg . . . to be in readiness for a great meeting, to commence at Cane Ridge shortly after. This

[1] "A Short History of the Life of Barton W. Stone, Written by Himself," in James R. Rogers, *The Cane Ridge Meeting-house* (Cincinnati: The Standard Publishing Co., 1910), pp. 157–162.

memorable meeting came on Thursday or Friday before the third Lord's Day in August, 1801. The roads were literally crowded with wagons, carriages, horsemen and footmen moving to the solemn camp. The sight was affecting. It was judged by military men on the ground that there were between twenty and thirty thousand collected. Four or five preachers were frequently speaking at the same time in different parts of the encampment, without confusion. The Methodist and Baptist preachers aided in the work, and all appeared cordially united in it — of one mind and one soul, and the salvation of sinners seemed to be the great object of all. We all engaged in singing the same songs of praise — all united in prayer — all preached the same things — free salvation urged upon all by faith and repentance. A particular description of this meeting would fill a large volume, and then the half would not be told. The numbers converted will be known only in eternity. Many things transpired there which were so much like miracles that, if they were not, they had the same effect as miracles on infidels and unbelievers; for many of them by these were convinced that Jesus was the Christ, and bowed in submission to him. This meeting continued six or seven days and nights, and would have continued longer, but provisions for such a multitude failed in the neighborhood.

To this meeting many had come from Ohio and other distant parts, who returned home and diffused the same spirit in their neighborhoods, and the same works followed. So low had religion sunk, and such carelessness universally had prevailed, that I have thought that nothing common could have arrested the attention of the world; therefore these uncommon agitations were sent for this purpose. However, this was their effect upon the community. As I have seen no history of these bodily agitations of that day, but from the pens of enemies or scorners, and as I have been an eye and ear witness of them from the beginning, and am now over threescore and ten years of age, on the brink of eternity, into which almost all of the old witnesses have entered, therefore I will endeavor to give a description of them in a distinct chapter, for your information.

Bodily Exercises in the Revival

The bodily agitations, or exercises, attending the excitement in the beginning of this century were various, and called by various names; as, the falling exercise, the jerks, the dancing exercise, the barking exercise, the laughing and singing exercise, etc. The falling exercise was very common among all classes, the saints and sinners of every age and of every grade, from the philosopher to the clown. The subject of this exercise would, generally, with a piercing scream, fall like a log on the floor, earth, or mud, and appear as dead. Of thousands of similar cases I will mention one. At a meeting two gay young ladies, sisters, were standing together attending to the exercises and preaching at the time. Instantly they both fell with a shriek of distress, and lay for more than an hour apparently in a lifeless state. Their mother, a pious Baptist, was in great distress, fearing they would not revive. At length they began to exhibit symptoms of life by crying fervently for mercy, and then relapsed into the same deathlike state with an awful gloom on their countenances. After awhile the gloom on the face of one was succeeded by a heavenly smile, and she cried out, "Precious Jesus!" and rose up and spoke of the love of God, the preciousness of Jesus, and of the glory of the gospel, to the surrounding crowd in language almost superhuman, and pathetically exhorted all to repentance. In a little while after the other sister was similarly exercised. From that time they became remarkably pious members of the church, and were constant in attendance. . . .

The jerks cannot be so easily described. Sometimes the subject of the jerks would be affected in some one member of the body, and sometimes in the whole system. When the head alone was affected, it would be jerked backward and forward, or from side to side, so quickly that the features of the face could not be distinguished. When the whole system was affected, I have seen the person stand in one place and jerk backward and forward in quick succession, their head nearly touching the floor behind and before. All classes, saints and sinners, the strong as well as the weak, were thus affected. I have inquired of those thus affected. They could not account for it; but some have told me that those were among the happiest seasons of their lives. I have seen some wicked persons thus affected, and all the time cursing the jerks, while they were thrown to the earth with violence. Though so awful to behold, I do not remember that any one of the thousands I have seen ever sustained an injury in body. This was as strange as the exercise itself.

The dancing exercise. This generally began with the jerks and was peculiar to professors of religion. The subject, after jerking awhile, began to dance, and then the jerks would cease. Such dancing was indeed heavenly to the spectators. There was nothing in it like levity nor calculated to excite levity in the beholders. The smile of heaven shone on the countenance of the subject, and assimilated to angels appeared the whole person. Sometimes the motion was quick and sometimes slow. Thus they continued to move forward and backward in the same track or alley till nature seemed exhausted, and they would fall prostrate on the floor or earth unless caught by those standing by. While thus exercised, I have heard their solemn praises and prayers ascending to God.

The barking exercise (as opposers contemptuously called it) was nothing but the jerks. A person affected with the jerks, especially in his head, would often make a grunt, or bark, if you please, from the suddenness of the jerk. This name of barking seems to have had its origin from an old Presbyterian preacher of East Tennessee. He had gone into the woods for private devotion and was seized with the jerks. Standing near a sapling, he caught hold of it to prevent his falling, and as his head jerked back he uttered a grunt or kind of noise similar to a bark, his face being turned upwards. Some wag discovered him in this position and reported that he found him barking up a tree.

The laughing exercise was frequent, confined solely with the religious. It was a loud, hearty laughter, but . . . it excited laughter in none else. The subject appeared rapturously solemn, and his laughter excited solemnity in saints and sinners. It is truly indescribable. . . .

I shall close this chapter with the singing exercise. This is more unaccountable than anything else I ever saw. The subject in a very happy state of mind would sing most melodiously, not from the mouth or nose, but entirely in the breast, the sounds issuing thence. Such music silenced everything and attracted the attention of all. It was most heavenly. None could ever be tired of hearing it. . . .

Thus have I given a brief account of the wonderful things that appeared in the great excitement in the beginning of this century. That there were many eccentricities and much fanaticism in this excitement, was acknowledged by its warmest advocates; indeed, it would have been a wonder if such things had not appeared in the circumstances of that time. Yet the good effects were seen and acknowledged in every neighborhood, and among the different sects it silenced contention and promoted unity for awhile; and these blessed effects would have continued had not men put forth their unhallowed hands to hold up their tottering ark, mistaking it for the ark of God.

THE REVIVALIST TRADITION: *Revivalism has been an important phenomenon throughout much of American history and has not been limited to any denomination or geographic area. Dwight L. Moody (left) combined evangelism with good business techniques to win converts in urban America.*

Revivalism also flourished in rural areas. Camp meetings, held in large tents or out of doors, often drew tens of thousands, as in the 1854 forest service pictured below. Such meetings afforded the opportunity for emotional and religious expression, as well as for many dramatic conversions. For some, the jerking exercise (right) signaled the moment of grace.

2. "New Measures" to Promote Revivals[1]

✢ *Charles G. Finney*

In the days of Jonathan Edwards, the activity of God in the salvation of sinners was shrouded in mystery, so that none might predict where or when the experience of conversion would be felt. In the nineteenth century, however, evangelicals assumed that conversions could be brought about by the use of tried and tested revivalistic techniques. Charles G. Finney (1792–1875) was one of the best known of the new generation of revivalists, and he developed such techniques as "protracted meetings" and the "anxious seat," which were exceedingly effective and widely copied. In his Lectures on Revivals of Religion *(1835), Finney defended his "new measures" against the criticisms of older revivalists.* ■

In the present generation, many things have been introduced which have proved useful, but have been opposed on the ground that they were innovations. And as many are still unsettled in regard to them, I have thought it best to make some remarks concerning them. There are three things in particular, which have chiefly attracted remark, and therefore I shall speak of them. They are *Anxious Meetings, Protracted Meetings,* and the *Anxious Seat.* These are all opposed, and are called new measures.

(1.) *Anxious Meetings.* The first that I ever heard of under that name was in New England, where they were appointed for the purpose of holding personal conversation with anxious sinners, and to adapt instruction to the cases of individuals so as to lead them immediately to Christ. The design of them is evidently philosophical, but they have been opposed because they were new. . . .

(2.) *Protracted Meetings.* These are not new, but have always been practised, in some form or other, ever since there was a church on earth. The Jewish festivals were nothing else but protracted meetings. In regard to the *manner,* they were conducted differently from what they are now. But the *design* was the same, to devote a series of days to religious services in order to make a more powerful

[1] Charles G. Finney, *Lectures on Revivals of Religion* (New York: Leavitt, Lord & Co., 1835), pp. 242, 244, 246–247.

impression of divine things upon the minds of the people. All denominations of Christians, when religion prospers among them, hold protracted meetings. . . .

God has a right to dispose of our time as he pleases, to require us to give up any portion of our time, or all our time, to duties of instruction and devotion. And when circumstances plainly call for it, it is our duty to lay aside every other business and make direct and continuous efforts for the salvation of souls. If we transact our business upon right principles and from right motives and wholly for the glory of God, we shall never object to go aside to attend a protracted meeting whenever there appears to be a call for it in the providence of God. . . . Whenever, therefore, you hear a man pleading that he cannot leave his business to attend a protracted meeting — that it is his duty to attend to business, there is reason to fear that he considers the business as his own, and the meeting as God's business. If he felt that the business of the store or farm was as much God's business as attending a protracted meeting, he would doubtless be very willing to rest from his worldly toils and go up to the house of God and be refreshed whenever there was an indication on the part of God that the community was called to that work. . . .

(3.) *The Anxious Seat.* By this I mean the appointment of some particular seat in the place of meeting, where the anxious may come and be addressed particularly and be made subjects of prayer, and sometimes conversed with individually. Of late this measure has met with more opposition than any of the others. What is the great objection? I cannot see it. . . .

When a person is seriously troubled in mind, everybody knows that there is a powerful tendency to try to keep it private that he is so, and it is a great thing to get the individual willing to have the fact known to others. And as soon as you can get him willing to make known his feelings, you have accomplished a great deal. When a person is borne down with a sense of his condition, if you can get him willing to have it known, if you can get him to break away from the chains of pride, you have gained an important point towards his conversion. This is agreeable to the philosophy of the human mind. How many thousands are there who will bless God to eternity that when pressed by the truth they were ever brought to take this step by which they threw off the idea that it was a dreadful thing to have anybody know that they were serious about their souls.

3. Home Missions on the Western Frontier[1]

✦ *Flavel Bascom*

As population moved westward, churches had to be estab-
lished in the new areas of settlement. The several denominations
organized home missionary societies to give financial assistance
and to provide ministerial leadership. Flavel Bascom, a graduate
of Yale, went to Illinois in 1833 as an agent of the American
Home Missionary Society, which was jointly sponsored by the
Congregationalists and the Presbyterians. His autobiography,
from which these passages are selected, was based on the diary he
kept at the time. ■

Early in my theological course I had my attention directed to the
claims of the West as a field of missionary labor. While I had been
absent from New Haven, several of my college friends, having entered the Theological Department, became particularly interested in
Illinois as a field of labor. They sought information. They met frequently for consultation, discussion, and prayer. They finally formed
themselves into a society, which has since been called the "New
Haven Band," pledging their co-operation in building up a Christian
college in this state and in planting Christian churches, and in promoting a true Christian civilization. When I was informed what they
were doing, the object enlisted my sympathies, and their plan commended itself to my judgment. After prayerful consideration, I was
persuaded to cast in my lot with them, making it my life work to aid
in educating and Christianizing the population of this new and
growing state.

Frontier Accommodations West of Chicago

Mr. Kirby's meeting house, in which I preached my second sermon
in Illinois, was made of logs, and consisted of two parts, an old and
new part. In the old part, the seats were made of rough slabs, and in
the new part, there being no floor, the sleepers were used for seats.
Men, women, and children in about equal proportions, and a good
supply of dogs, made up the congregation, and the preacher and the

[1] "The Autobiography of Flavel Bascom" in William Warren Sweet, *Religion*
on the American Frontier, 1783–1850, Vol. III (Chicago: University of Chicago
Press, 1939), pp. 234–235, 245, 257–259.

singers were not the only ones whose voices were heard in the assembly. The pulpit was made by setting two posts in the ground about four feet apart and on the top of these nailing a board, for the support of Bible and hymn book. Behind this a seat for the preacher was made by boring two holes in one of the logs in the end of the house, and inserting two pins horizontally, on which a rough board was placed. This was a very primitive style of architecture, but the place was far in advance of many houses in which I subsequently preached the Gospel.

Pioneer Preaching

My accommodations at home and my labors abroad were very unfavorable to such habits of study as a young minister needs [for] . . . intellectual growth and [for] the accumulation of resources for his work. The books required were not within my reach. The time to use them I could not command, and I had no place for solitary and uninterrupted study. But the customs and tastes of the people did not require written discourses nor elaborate preparation. The man who could get up and talk with the most freedom and fluency was listened to with the greatest admiration, without regard to the soundness of his logic or the literary polish of his style. I endeavored to draw sound instruction from the word of God, and present it in my discourses in a familiar and earnest way, so that I might secure attention, awaken interest, stimulate thought and study, and thus correct the erroneous notions so prevalent around us, and make the way of salvation so plain to my hearers that they need not err therein. And the result of my preaching was to dispel the mists and fogs in which ignorant and erroneous preachers had enveloped the minds of the people and to create a demand for a more thoughtful and less boisterous address from religious teachers. . . .

But there was a class of early settlers from Kentucky that were not easily reconciled to the change. Their feelings were expressed at one time in my hearing. I had preached at the log school house in Pleasant Grove on a certain Sabbath and had been immediately followed by a preacher of the early pioneer sort. He commenced by saying that his text was a passage which had come to his mind while the brother was speaking, *viz.*, "we have this treasure of the gospel in earthen vessels," etc. This passage, said he, teaches man's [inability] to keep the commandments of God. Having thus expounded it, he never referred to it again, but commenced an indiscriminate quotation of passages from the Genesis to Revelations and back again, with apparently no connection between them except that some word in one verse would serve as a catchword to remind him of another. Thus he went bellowing and blowing through the Bible shedding no more light upon the passages quoted than the roar of artillery does on our Declaration of Independence. But after service, as I was walking toward my horse and buggy, I heard two women before me discussing the sermons. In reference to the last, one of them said she "allowed that was the greatest sermon ever preached in that house." "Yes," replied the other, "but I don't like these Yankee preachers. They are always proving things, just like lawyers." And thus I labored on, trying to teach the people to "prove all things and hold fast that which is good."

4. Foreign Missionary Beginnings[1]

✤ Francis Wayland

While some missionaries were evangelizing the western frontier, others undertook to convert the heathen overseas. Foremost among them was Adoniram Judson, who sailed in 1812 with his wife for Burma. Originally a Congregationalist sent out under the auspices of the American Board of Commissioners for Foreign Missions, founded 1810, Judson became a Baptist en route, and his work was thenceforward supported by the newly-formed Baptist Triennial Convention. The author of this account of his work, Francis Wayland, was president of Brown University. ■

Mr. Judson having now arrived in Rangoon, the principal seaport of Burma, that portion of the heathen world to which the labors of his future life were to be devoted, it may be worth while to pause for a moment, to consider definitely the object which so exclusively controlled every energy of his soul. His life was unique and consistent, bearing upon one point, and ever striving to realize a single conception. When we know the principles which he embraced and the manner in which he felt obliged to carry them into practice, we are at once enabled to estimate his character, and take a just view of his services. . . .

[1] Francis Wayland, *A Memoir of the Life and Labors of the Rev. Adoniram Judson, D.D.* (Boston: Phillips, Sampson & Co., 1853), Vol. I, pp. 154, 156–157, 163.

Mr. Judson believed himself to be a disciple of Christ, saved from condemnation through the merits of the atonement; he acknowledged his personal obligation to obey this last command of his ascended Redeemer; nay, more, he was satisfied that he had been called to devote his life to this service. Holding such a belief, and acknowledging such obligations, he consecrated his whole being to the work, and with this consecration he allowed nothing else whatever to interfere.

The providence of God clearly directed him to the empire of Burma. He felt assured that he was thus sent, as the herald of Christ, to preach the gospel of peace to this benighted people. There was not, at the time of his arrival at Rangoon, a single native who had embraced the religion of Jesus. He was aware of the oppression and cruelty of the rulers, and of the wickedness and misery of the people; he knew that they were steeped in an idolatry that had become venerable by antiquity; yet he believed that in the gospel there existed the sovereign remedy for all these evils. He doubted not that when the gospel should be preached, the sinful nature of men would be transformed into the holy image of Christ; that every convert would become a center of moral illumination, that thus, by its own inherent power of indefinite expansion, the gospel would spread on every side among the people, until the temples of Gautama [Buddha] should be deserted, the moral character of men be renewed, and Burma become a kingdom of our Lord and of his Christ.

His object, then, was to accomplish the most stupendous revolution of which we can conceive in this whole people; it was nothing less than an entire transformation of the moral character of every individual. The means by which this was to be accomplished was very simple. It was the announcement of the message from God to man, attended by the omnipotent power of the Spirit of God. He believed that this work would thus be accomplished simply because God had promised it.

But while Mr. Judson felt that *his* appropriate field was Burma, and nothing but Burma, he gave to this field no peculiar pre-eminence. The whole heathen world was always in his view. He was ever suggesting to the board new fields of labor, and he was constantly bringing before the mercy seat in his most retired hours of devotion particular nations who had not yet attracted the attention of the friends of missions. Thus, at Maulmain he was always urging his brethren, and specially those whom he most highly esteemed and whose society he most enjoyed, to establish new missions in neighboring unevangelized countries. In no case, however, did he propose any labor to them which he was not willing to undertake himself. He desired that every one of them, as far as possible, should be a new center of gospel light, and he wished such centers to be multiplied as widely as possible. If the station at Maulmain has been the means of diffusing the knowledge of salvation to other and distant regions of India, this result has been owing, I apprehend, more to Dr. Judson's counsels, labors, and prayers than to those of any other individual.

5. America's Millennial Expectations[1]

✦ William Cogswell

American religion has tended to be activist rather than contemplative, and so Americans who looked forward to the Millennium assumed that they had to be active in ushering it in. Hence Finney's revivals were deliberately promoted, and home and foreign missionary societies were carefully organized. How all these activities were related was made clear in a book entitled The Harbinger of the Millennium, *by William Cogswell, the Secretary of the American Education Society, which was one of the benevolent societies organized by the evangelicals.* ■

No person who peruses the sacred Scriptures with attention and diligence can remain unconvinced that a period is approaching in which the Church of God in this world will enjoy far greater prosperity and happiness than it ever yet has done. This blessed season, technically called the Millennium, the Lord will hasten in his time. Those individuals who desire, pray, and labor for the advancement of this blessed day are coworkers with him in bringing it forward, and all those Christian enterprises which serve to introduce it may be considered as harbingers of its approach. Such are the various benevolent societies whose object is to diffuse religious knowledge and instruction. They are combined instruments in promoting the conversion of the world and the salvation of men. They have an interest in each other, depend upon each other, and assist each other. There is no occasion for collision or rivalship among them. They are each of

[1] William Cogswell, *The Harbinger of the Millennium* (Boston: Peirce and Parker, 1833), pp. iii, 299–300.

them important—and most of them absolutely necessary. They hasten the accomplishment of that glorious and animating prediction: "They shall all know me, from the least of them unto the greatest of them, saith the Lord." These are precursors and will usher in the latter-day glory as the morning stars precede the natural sun and usher in the natural day. As this period advances, that system of benevolent operations which is designed to enlighten and bless the world will increase in extension and efficiency.

Work Still to be Done

Far greater things in religion must be attempted and accomplished than ever yet have been.

The Bible, that great Magna Charta of the liberties, peace, happiness, and salvation of man must be imparted to all the destitute. Heralds of the cross must be raised up and sent forth to publish the glad tidings of mercy to all people under heaven. The Saviour's mandate, "Go ye into all the world, and preach the gospel to every creature," given eighteen centuries ago to his disciples, will yet be obeyed. Will any say this cannot be done? It can — it will be done. As a pledge of this, we have the purpose, covenant, veracity, perfections and word of God. This great work, then, will be accomplished. . . . The Lord will spread the triumphs of the cross. Soon the whole earth will chant the praises of the Redeemer, and the song of salvation will echo from shore to shore. But in order to [do] this there must be more fervent prayer, more abundant labors, more enlarged charities. In the conquest of the world to Christ, the church must become a well-disciplined army, and every member of it must know his place and duty. There must be a mighty onset against sin and Satan. In this war, Christians must enlist for actual service, and for life. Is it said this is enthusiasm? Be it so. There never was a great and noble enterprise accomplished without enthusiasm. But is not this proselytism, sectarianism? This we acknowledge to be a fact, but to what, and to whom do we proselyte and divide? To the Christian religion, and to the sect of Christ. In this blessed work let us become enthusiastic. For Christ let us make proselytes. For the conversion of the world to him, let us pray, and labor, till our Master call us to our rest. Then, though we should not while here on the earth see the day of millennial blessedness, we shall be permitted to look down from the battlements of heaven, and behold all this world in complete subjection to Jesus Christ.

VI. Variant Forms of Dissent

Those who disagreed with the main thrust of evangelical Protestantism were not all cast in the same mold. Some of them held a more optimistic view of human nature, asserting men's inherent capacity to grow in righteousness. Some rejected revivalism on the grounds that emotionalism manipulated by the revivalist is not the same thing as piety. Some argued for a more churchly concept of the Christian community and a more formal or even ritualistic kind of worship. Some found themselves marked as distrusted minorities, either persecuted or under pressure to conform. These various religious groups, however widely they differed among themselves, had in common the need to understand themselves, at least in part, in terms of the way in which they dissented from the dominant thrust of evangelical religion in America. ■

1. Liberal Christianity[1]

✤ William Ellery Channing

The religious liberalism for which John Bass was an early spokesman became increasingly important, especially in eastern Massachusetts, emerging as Unitarianism in the nineteenth century. It rejected the prevailing orthodox doctrine of human sinfulness and the emphasis of the evangelicals on revivalism and conversions. The response of the evangelicals was to try to isolate the liberals and to deny them the Christian name. In 1815, William Ellery Channing (1780–1842), the best known and most widely respected leader of the liberals, protested this "system of exclusion and denunciation" in religion. ■

[1] *The Works of William E. Channing, D.D.* (Boston: James Munroe & Co., 1841), Vol. V, pp. 373, 374, 376, 381–382.

Nothing is plainer than that the leaders of the party called "Orthodox" have adopted and mean to enforce a system of exclusion in regard to Liberal Christians. They spare no pains to infect the minds of their too easy followers with the persuasion that they ought to refuse communion with their Unitarian brethren, and to deny them the name, character, and privileges of Christians. . . .

Why are the name, character, and rights of Christians to be denied to Unitarians? Do they deny that Jesus is the Christ? Do they reject his word as the rule of their faith and practice? Do their lives discover indifference to his authority and example? No, these are not their offences. They are deficient in none of the qualifications of disciples which were required in the primitive age. Their offence is that they read the Scriptures for themselves and derive from them different opinions on certain points from those which others have adopted. Mistake of judgment is their pretended crime, and this crime is laid to their charge by men who are as liable to mistake as themselves, and who seem to them to have fallen into some of the grossest errors. A condemning sentence from such judges carries with it no terror. Sorrow for its uncharitableness, and strong disapprobation of its arrogance are the principal feelings which it inspires.

In vindication of this system of exclusion and denunciation it is often urged that the "honor of religion," the "purity of the church," and the "cause of truth" forbid those who hold the true Gospel to maintain fellowship with those who support corrupt and injurious opinions. Without stopping to notice the modesty of those who claim an exclusive knowledge of the true Gospel, I would answer that the "honor of religion" can never suffer by admitting to Christian fellowship men of irreproachable lives, whilst it has suffered most severely from that narrow and uncharitable spirit which has excluded such men for imagined errors. I answer again, that the "cause of truth" can never suffer by admitting to Christian fellowship men who honestly profess to make the Scriptures their rule of faith and practice, whilst it has suffered most severely by substituting for this standard conformity to human creeds and formularies.

Evil Consequences of Intolerance

Many other considerations may be added to those which have been already urged against the system of excluding from Christian fellowship men of upright lives on account of their opinions. It necessarily generates perpetual discord in the church. Men differ in opinions as much as in features. No two minds are perfectly accordant. The shades of belief are infinitely diversified. Amidst this immense variety of sentiment every man is right in his own eyes. Every man discovers errors in the creed of his brother. Every man is prone to magnify the importance of his own peculiarities and to discover danger in the peculiarities of others. This is human nature. Every man is partial to his own opinions because they are his own, and his self-will and pride are wounded by contradiction. Now what must we expect when beings so erring, so divided in sentiment, and so apt to be unjust to the views of others assert the right of excluding one another from the Christian church on account of imagined error? As the Scriptures confine this right to no individual and to no body of Christians, it belongs alike to all; and what must we expect, when Christians of all capacities and dispositions, the ignorant, prejudiced, and self-conceited, imagine it their duty to prescribe opinions to Christendom, and to open or to shut the door of the church according to the decision which their neighbors may form on some of the most perplexing points of theology? This question, unhappily, has received answer upon answer in ecclesiastical history. We there see Christians denouncing and excommunicating one another for supposed error, until every denomination has been pronounced accursed by some portion of the Christian world; so that were the curses of men to prevail, not one human being would enter heaven. To me it appears that to plead for the right of excluding men of blameless lives on account of their opinions is to sound the peal of perpetual and universal war. . . . Never will there be peace until Christians agree to differ, and agree to look for the evidences of Christian character in the temper and the life.

2. Christian Nurture[1]

✦ *Horace Bushnell*

Even within the predominantly evangelical denominations, there were those who criticized some of the assumptions of evangelical religion. Among Congregationalists, the most im-

[1] Horace Bushnell, *Christian Nurture* (New York: Charles Scribner, 1861), pp. 10, 30–31, 59–61.

portant of these was Horace Bushnell of Hartford, Connecticut (1802–1876). He rejected the prevailing emphasis on revivalism, and argued that for the creation of Christian character, reliance should be placed on family training in childhood much more than on sudden conversion later on. Vigorously attacked in his own day, Bushnell nevertheless contributed a great deal to the development of religious liberalism by the younger men of the next generation. ■

Assuming then the question above stated, What is the true idea of Christian education? I answer in the following proposition, which it will be the aim of my argument to establish, *viz*:

That the child is to grow up a Christian, and never know himself as being otherwise.

In other words, the aim, effort, and expectation should be not as is commonly assumed, that the child is to grow up in sin, to be converted after he comes to a mature age; but that he is to open on the world as one that is spiritually renewed, not remembering the time when he went through a technical experience, but seeming rather to have loved what is good from his earliest years. . . .

He is never at any moment after birth to be regarded as perfectly beyond the sphere of good and bad exercises; for the parent exercises himself in the child, playing his emotions and sentiments and working a character in him by virtue of an organic power.

And this is the very idea of Christian education, that it begins with nurture or cultivation. And the intention is that the Christian life and spirit of the parents, which are in and by the Spirit of God, shall flow into the mind of the child, to blend with his incipient and half-formed exercises; that they shall thus beget their own good within him — their thoughts, opinions, faith, and love, which are to become a little more, and yet a little more, his own separate exercise, but still the same in character. The contrary assumption, that virtue must be the product of separate and absolutely independent choice, is pure assumption. As regards the measure of personal merit and demerit, it is doubtless true that every subject of God is to be responsible only for what is his own. But virtue still is rather a *state* of being than an act or series of acts; and if we look at the causes which induce or prepare such a state, the will of the person himself may have a part among these causes more or less important, and it works no absurdity to suppose that one may be even prepared to such a state by causes prior to his own will; so that when he sets off to act for himself, his struggle and duty may be rather to sustain and perfect the state begun, than to produce a new one. Certain it is that we are never at any age so independent as to be wholly out of the reach of organic laws which affect our character.

Critique of Revivalism

. . . It is to be deeply considered in connection with this view of family nurture whether it does not meet many of the deficiencies we deplore in the Christian character of our times and the present state of our churches. We have been expecting to thrive too much by conquest and too little by growth. I desire to speak with all caution of what are very unfortunately called revivals of religion; for, apart from the name, which is modern, and from certain crudities and excesses that go with it — which name, crudities, and excesses are wholly adventitious as regards the substantial merits of such scenes — apart from these, I say, there is abundant reason to believe that God's spiritual economy includes varieties of exercise, answering in all important respects to these visitations of mercy so much coveted in our churches. They are needed. A perfectly uniform demonstration in religion is not possible or desirable. . . .

But the difficulty is with us that we idolize such scenes, and make them the whole of our religion. We assume that nothing good is doing or can be done at any other time. And what is even worse, we often look upon these scenes and desire them rather as scenes of victory than of piety. They are the harvest-times of conversion, and conversion is too nearly everything with us. In particular we see no way to gather in disciples save by means of certain marked experiences, developed in such scenes in adult years. Our very children can possibly come to no good save in this way. Instrumentalities are invented to compass our object that are only mechanical, and the hope of mere present effect is supposed to justify them. Present effect, in the view of many, justifies anything and everything. We strain every nerve of motion, exhaust every capacity of endurance, and push on till nature sinks in exhaustion. We preach too much and live Christ too little. We do many things which in a cooler mood are seen to hurt the dignity of religion and which somewhat shame and sicken ourselves. Hence the present state of religion in our country. We have worked a vein till it has run out. The churches are exhausted.[2] There

[2] This was written, I believe, in the year A.D. 1846 [Bushnell's note].

is little to attract them when they look upon the renewal of scenes through which many of them have passed. They look about them, with a sigh, to ask if possibly there is no better way, and some are ready to find that better way in a change of their religion. Nothing different from this ought to have been expected. No nation can long thrive by a spirit of conquest; no more can a church. There must be an internal growth that is made by holy industry in the common walks of life and duty.

3. Controversy Among the Episcopalians[1]
✚ William Croswell

In the Episcopal Church, criticism of evangelicalism came from "High Churchmen." They stressed formality and order in worship rather than the spontaneous prayer of revival meetings, the Church and its sacraments as the channels of God's redeeming grace rather than the experience of conversion, and the historic continuity of the Church as a divinely ordained institution rather than the churches as voluntary assemblages of the faithful. To Low Churchmen, all this seemed suspiciously like Roman Catholicism. The passage that follows describes an unhappy episode when a low-church bishop realized that one of the churches in his diocese was explicitly high church in its sympathies. The bishop was the Reverend Manton Eastburn of Massachusetts; the church was the Church of the Advent in Boston, of which the Reverend William Croswell was the rector. ■

The Bishop Comes to a Confirmation Service

The Right Rev. the Bishop of the diocese visited the Church of the Advent, by appointment, for the purpose of administering confirmation, on Sunday evening, November 23, 1845. The rector and his assistant were in the robing room when the bishop arrived. The usual civilities were exchanged, and there was no apparent want of courtesy or good will on the part of the bishop. . . . On entering the chancel, the bishop went to the right end of the holy table, and I

---

[1] [Harry Croswell], *A Memoir of the Late Rev. William Croswell, D.D.* (New York: D. Appleton & Co., 1854), pp. 353–356.

offered evening prayer at the other. The Rev. Mr. Pollard, who was on the same side of the chancel with myself — and whose duty it was to read the lesson for the evening from the lectern — knelt down during the prayers with his face towards the corner of the holy table.

The chapel was crowded and the air was close and oppressive. The interest in the services was somewhat exciting to me, and, as I supposed at the time, affected the bishop in the same way. Seventeen candidates were presented, all of them of mature years; and all of them were at the time, or have since become, communicants. There was no sermon. In the place of it, the bishop, after the confirmation, returned to the right of the holy table, and standing with his back nearly against the wall, delivered an extemporaneous address. There was a hurry and agitation of manner which I attributed at the time to interest in the duty before him.

The Bishop Rebukes "Superstition"

After the congregation had begun to retire, I went over to the side of the chancel, where the bishop was standing and wiping the perspiration from his face, and made some allusion to the heat. . . . To this he replied by an impatient waving of his hand towards the windows, as if they should have been further let down. After the aisles were further cleared, I told the bishop that we could then get to the robing room at the opposite end, if he wished. He said that he did not like to expose himself to a change of air until he was cooler, or something to that effect. Presently he said, with an abruptness and severity of manner that startled me, "Mr. Pollard, what did you say *Saint* Titus for? Why can't you say *Titus*, as everybody else does?"

Mr. Pollard said he did not know but others said as he did.

Bishop. "No, sir, never. The apostles are called saints, and no others. We don't say *Saint* Mary. . . . And why do you kneel in that way, half a mile off from the table? I have spoken to you often enough about these mummeries, at Nantucket. These things give pious people great offence."

Pollard. "How would you have me kneel, sir?"

Bishop. "Turn to your chair, and kneel there."

I then said, "Bishop, Mr. [Pollard] kneels according to our ordinary usage." . . . The bishop expressed great surprise, as if he had heard of this for the first time.

Bishop. "Mr. Croswell, I am very much surprised at this. I should

not have expected it of you. What is the use and meaning of it? Why
kneel down half a mile off, and not come up at once to the table? I
can understand why a Romish [Roman Catholic] priest should do so.
The host is there. But what have we on the table to worship?"

I spoke of my conviction that our method ministered to reverence.
Bishop. "I think as much of reverence as any one, but I abhor
superstition!"

The Bishop Leaves, Not to Return

The bishop called attention to our large cross, candlesticks, shelf,
etc., as indicative of affinities with Rome. "If an Irishman were to
come in here," said he, "and see that cross, he would kneel down to
it at once, in the aisle. He would think that he was in a Roman
Catholic chapel. It looks like one." I said that I thought, without
the "Roman," his remark was true. "It certainly did look like a
Catholic chapel." ...

The bishop then being ready to leave, I was unwilling to part with
him thus, on an occasion from which I had anticipated so much satisfaction. I said, "Bishop, I thank you for your services this evening,
which have afforded us great gratification." To this he responded, as
we shook hands — but with some hesitation — "Well, I hope God
will prosper you."

This was the substance of our conversation on that evening, when
our joy was suddenly turned into heaviness.

4. "American Lutheranism" Rejected[1]

✤ William J. Mann

*In the early decades of the nineteenth century, many Lutherans
in this country were influenced by the modes of thought and
revivalistic practises of evangelical Protestantism. The term
"American Lutheranism" came to be used to refer to this
tendency. Later in the century, under the impact of large-scale
migration from Germany, there was a reaction against this American Lutheranism. The passage that follows is an expression of*

[1] William J. Mann, *Lutheranism in America* (Philadelphia: Lindsay & Blakis-
ton, 1857), pp. 18–19, 27–28, 37.

*this reaction; in it, the author uses the term "Puritan" to char-
acterize what we have been describing as evangelical Protestantism.* ■

It is a settled fact in the minds of a large majority of the Americans
that America is animated by an entirely new, peculiar, and more
perfect political, social, and religious life. In this latter, religious life,
with which we have principally to do, they regard their own as being
far in advance of every other country — an opinion which neither
the contradictory testimony of the actual condition of private and
public life, nor, or rather far less, a more intimate acquaintance with
the religious condition of Europe, will ever be likely to change. It is
well known how often Europeans have been deceived in their first
impressions of the showy piety of this country, until they were able
to look below the surface and make themselves acquainted with
things as they really are.

The prominent character of Protestant piety in this country is, as
is well known, Puritanic. The Puritans have put the impress of their
energetic spiritual nature upon centuries and generations. The
strength of their system lies in its deep-toned moral earnestness, its
weakness in a one-sided, extremely limited view in matters pertaining
to religion; in consequence of which they look upon themselves as
having attained the utmost limit of the purity of Christian doctrine
and practice, whilst they reject, in the most summary manner, whatever either is really Romish, or by them supposed to be so. However
strongly marked the points of difference between the primitive Puritans, Quakers, Baptists, Presbyterians, and others, originally have
been, or in many at present may be, and however dissimilar their
forms, manner of worship, government and discipline, the practical
religious spirit of all will be found substantially the same, and this is
the prevailing spirit of American piety.

"Puritan" Influence on Lutheranism

One reason, among many, why we are not surprised at the over-
powering influence which Puritanism has exerted over Lutheranism
is, because from it the *religious life* of the Lutheran Church in this
country has for the last fifty years received its main impulse. Puritanism itself is much less theory than life, activity and effect. This, its

strength, it at one time exhibited in a spirit of fanaticism towards everything Romish, as against everything anti-Christian in a special sense. It has conquered the ground it occupies, and endeavors to maintain it in the New World. During the last century it found an ally in Methodism. . . . With the exception of some few matters pertaining to church organization, they agree with one another most admirably. What Puritanism in doctrine and worship rejects as unchristian, Methodism rejects likewise; whilst the mode and manner in which the Methodist incites to religious life is, in turn, not at all foreign to the Puritan. This Puritanic-Methodistic-English Protestantism has most powerfully influenced the English portion of the Lutheran Church in this country.

"Puritanism" Rejected

The impression is gaining ground among our ministers and laity that the Lutheran Church has an individual character in regard to church usages and confession, and that this character she ought not to forfeit. There is an increasing conviction that the Lutheran Church only shows its weakness by becoming the sport of Puritanical and Methodistical religious tendencies.

5. Westward to Zion[1]

✣ *Thomas L. Kane*

The Church of Jesus Christ of Latter-Day Saints, commonly referred to as the Mormon Church, was wholly American in origin. In this respect, it differed from most American religious bodies, which were transplanted from Europe. The experience of the Mormons in moving westward to settle on the frontier was characteristically American, as was their intention to create a new Zion. Yet other Americans were disturbed by their innovations in doctrine and worship, and feared the influence, political and other, that might be exerted by a cohesive minority. So the Mormons became increasingly a "peculiar people," surrounded by distrustful or hostile "gentiles." Persecuted in Missouri and

[1] Thomas L. Kane, *The Mormons* (Philadelphia: King & Baird, 1850), pp. 3–11.

Illinois, they began in 1846 the migration overland to the valley of the Great Salt Lake, leaving behind the deserted city of Nauvoo, described below. The author of the passage was Thomas L. Kane, not himself a Mormon, but sympathetic with them in their plight. ■

A few years ago, ascending the Upper Mississippi in the autumn, when its waters were low, I was compelled to travel by land past the region of the Rapids. My road lay through the Half-Breed Tract, a fine section of Iowa, which the unsettled state of its land-titles had appropriated as a sanctuary for coiners, horse thieves, and other outlaws. I had left my steamer at Keokuk, at the foot of the Lower Fall, to hire a carriage and to contend for some fragments of a dirty meal with the swarming flies, the only scavengers of the locality. From this place to where the deep water of the river returns, my eye wearied to see everywhere sordid, vagabond and idle settlers; and a country marred, without being improved, by their careless hands.

I was descending the last hillside upon my journey when a landscape in delightful contrast broke upon my view. Half encircled by a bend of the river, a beautiful city lay glittering in the fresh morning sun; its bright new dwellings, set in cool green gardens, ranging up around a stately dome-shaped hill, which was crowned by a noble marble edifice whose high tapering spire was radiant with white and gold. The city appeared to cover several miles; and beyond it, in the background, there rolled off a fair country, checkered by the careful lines of fruitful husbandry. The unmistakeable marks of industry, enterprise, and educated wealth everywhere made the scene one of singular and most striking beauty.

The Deserted City

It was a natural impulse to visit this inviting region. I procured a skiff, and rowing across the river, landed at the chief wharf of the city. No one met me there. I looked, and saw no one. I could hear no one move; though the quiet everywhere was such that I heard the flies buzz, and the water ripples break against the shallow of the beach. I walked through the solitary streets. The town lay as in a dream, under some deadening spell of loneliness from which I almost feared to wake it. For plainly it had not slept long. There was no grass growing up in the paved ways. Rains had not entirely washed away the prints of dusty footsteps.

Yet I went about unchecked. I went into empty workshops, rope-walks, and smithies. The spinner's wheel was idle; the carpenter had gone from his workbench and shavings, his unfinished sash and casing. Fresh bark was in the tanner's vat, and the fresh-chopped lightwood stood piled against the baker's oven. The blacksmith's shop was cold; but his coal heap and ladling pool and crooked water horn were all there as if he had just gone off for a holiday. No work people anywhere looked to know my errand. If I went into the gardens, clinking the wicket latch loudly after me, to pull the marygolds, heart's-ease, and lady-slippers, and draw a drink with the water sodden well-bucket and its noisy chain; or, knocking off with my stick the tall heavy-headed dahlias and sunflowers, hunted over the beds for cucumbers and love apples, no one called out to me from any opened window, or dog sprang forward to bark an alarm. I could have supposed the people hidden in the houses, but the doors were unfastened; and when at last I timidly entered them, I found dead ashes white upon the hearths, and had to tread a tiptoe, as if walking down the aisle of a country church, to avoid rousing irreverent echoes from the naked floors.

On the outskirts of the town was the city graveyard. But there was no record of plague there, nor did it in any wise differ much from other Protestant American cemeteries. Some of the mounds were not long sodded; some of the stones were newly set, their dates recent, and their black inscriptions glossy in the mason's hardly dried lettering ink. Beyond the graveyard, out in the fields, I saw, in one spot hard by where the fruited boughs of a young orchard had been roughly torn down, the still smoldering embers of a barbecue fire that had been constructed of rails from the fencing round it. It was the latest sign of life there. Fields upon fields of heavy-headed yellow grain lay rotting ungathered upon the ground. No one was at hand to take in their rich harvest. As far as the eye could reach, they stretched away — they, sleeping too in the hazy air of autumn.

The Invaders

Only two portions of the city seemed to suggest the import of this mysterious solitude. On the southern suburb the houses looking out upon the country showed by their splintered woodwork and walls battered to the foundation that they had lately been the mark of a destructive cannonade. And in and around the splendid temple, which had been the chief object of my admiration, armed men were barracked, surrounded by their stacks of musketry and pieces of heavy ordnance. These challenged me to render an account of myself, and why I had had the temerity to cross the water without a written permit from a leader of their band.

Though these men were generally more or less under the influence of ardent spirits, after I had explained myself as a passing stranger, they seemed anxious to gain my good opinion. They told me the story of the dead city: that it had been a notable manufacturing and commercial mart sheltering over 20,000 persons; that they had waged war with its inhabitants for several years, and had been finally successful, only a few days before my visit, in an action fought in front of the ruined suburb, after which they had driven them forth at the point of the sword. The defence, they said, had been obstinate, but gave way on the third day's bombardment. They boasted greatly of their prowess, especially in this battle, as they called it; but I discovered they were not of one mind as to certain of the exploits that had distinguished it, one of which, as I remember, was that they had slain a father and his son, a boy of fifteen, not long residents of the fated city, whom they admitted to have borne a character without reproach.

They also conducted me inside the massive sculptured walls of the curious temple in which they said the banished inhabitants were accustomed to celebrate the mystic rites of an unhallowed worship. They particularly pointed out to me certain features of the building, which having been the peculiar objects of a former superstitious regard, they had as matter of duty sedulously defiled and defaced. The reputed sites of certain shrines they had thus particularly noticed, and various sheltered chambers, in one of which was a deep well, constructed they believed with a dreadful design. Beside these, they led me to see a large and deep chiseled marble vase or basin, supported upon twelve oxen, also of marble, and of the size of life, of which they told some romantic stories. They said the deluded persons, most of whom were immigrants from a great distance, believed their deity countenanced their reception here of a baptism of regeneration, as proxies for whomsoever they held in warm affection in the countries from which they had come; that here parents "went into the water" for their lost children, children for their parents, widows for their spouses, and young persons for their lovers, that thus the Great Vase came to be for them associated with all dear and distant memories, and was therefore the object, of all others in the building, to which they attached the greatest degree of idolatrous affection. On this account the victors had so diligently desecrated it as to render the apartment in which it was contained too noisome to abide in. . . .

The Refugees

It was after nightfall, when I was ready to cross the river on my return. The wind had freshened since the sunset, and the water beating roughly into my little boat, I headed higher up the stream than the point I had left in the morning, and landed where a faint glimmering light invited me to steer.

Here among the dock and rushes, sheltered only by the darkness, without roof between them and the sky, I came upon a crowd of several hundred human creatures, whom my movements roused from uneasy slumber upon the ground. . . .

Dreadful indeed was the suffering of these forsaken beings. Cowed and cramped by cold and sunburn, alternating as each weary day and night dragged on, they were, almost all of them, the crippled victims of disease. They were there because they had no homes, nor hospital nor poorhouse nor friends to offer them any. They could not satisfy the feeble cravings of their sick, they had not bread to quiet the fractious hunger cries of their children. Mothers and babes, daughters and grandparents, all of them alike were bivouacked in tatters, wanting even covering to comfort those whom the sick shiver of fever was searching to the marrow.

These were Mormons, famishing, in Lee county, Iowa, in the fourth week of the month of September, in the year of our Lord 1846. The city . . . was Nauvoo, Illinois. The Mormons were the owners of that city, and the smiling country round. And those who had stopped their ploughs, who had silenced their hammers, their axes, their shuttles and their workshop wheels; those who had put out their fires, who had eaten their food, spoiled their orchards, and trampled under foot their thousands of acres of unharvested bread; these were the keepers of their dwellings, the carousers in their temple — whose drunken riot insulted the ears of their dying. . . .

They were, all told, not more than six hundred and forty persons who were thus lying on the river flats. But the Mormons in Nauvoo and its dependencies had been numbered the year before at over twenty thousand. Where were they? They had last been seen carrying in mournful trains their sick and wounded, halt and blind, to disappear behind the western horizon, pursuing the phantom of another home. Hardly anything else was known of them, and people asked with curiosity what had been their fate, what their fortunes.

6. Catholicism and the Public Schools[1]

✤ Commonwealth v. Cooke

As the Roman Catholic minority grew in numbers, its presence was felt as a threat by many Protestants, especially since most Catholics were recent immigrants. The resulting clash of cultures was sharply felt in the field of education. The Protestant majority argued that the role of the common schools was to educate children for responsible citizenship, not to inculcate sectarian beliefs. But the Catholics complained that the atmosphere in the schools was really thoroughly Protestant and sectarian, giving the impression that only Protestantism was compatible with good citizenship. The court decision that follows resulted from the refusal of a Catholic schoolboy to recite the Ten Commandments in the usual Protestant version. ■

Facts of the Case

The complaint in this case was made on the 16th day of March last, and charges that "McLaurin F. Cooke, teacher, on the 14th day of March, 1859, committed an assault and battery on Thomas J. Wall, son of the complainant, under circumstances of aggravation; that Thomas was eleven years of age, a pupil in the Eliot School, and defendant a teacher, and that defendant struck, beat and wounded Thomas with a stick for the space of thirty minutes, inflicting serious wounds."

Upon this complaint a warrant was issued by order of court, the

---

[1] Commonwealth v. Cooke. Police Court of Boston, Massachusetts, 1859, 7 Am. L. Reg. 417.

defendant Cooke arrested, and in open court pleaded not guilty to the complaint.

Upon this issue, evidence was introduced on the part of the Commonwealth to prove the assault, and by the defendant explanatory of the matter, and from the evidence so introduced the following facts appeared:

That the defendant was the first assistant teacher in the Eliot School, Samuel W. Mason, Principal; that Thomas J. Wall was a scholar in said school, and had been for six or seven years last past. That during his attendance the Bible in the common English version[2] was read in the school, and that the scholars sufficiently advanced were required to read or commit to memory the Lord's Prayer and the Ten Commandments.

That by the rules and regulations of the school, the Commandments were repeated by the scholars every Monday morning, and that the boy Wall had repeated them without objection until Monday, March the 7th, when he refused, and was discharged from the school. That an interview was had between the father of the boy and the principal of the school, and the boy returned to the school.

That on Monday, the 14th of March, he refused again to read or repeat the Commandments, giving as reasons for so doing, that his father had agreed with Mr. Mason that he should not say them. That his father had told him for his life not to say them, and that his priest had also told him not to say them, and that on the Sunday previous to the 14th the priest (Father Wiget), while addressing nine hundred children of St. Mary's Church, of whom Wall was one, told them not to be cowards to their religion, and not to read or repeat the Commandments in school, that if they did he would read their names from the altar.

That Wall came to the school on Monday with the determination not to read or repeat them. . . .

It further appeared from the evidence that there was a concerted plan of action on Monday the 14th between many of the boys to refuse to obey the orders of the school if required to read or repeat the Lord's Prayer or the Commandments, and that two-thirds of the scholars composing the school where Wall attended, and numbering

[2] [**common English version:** the King James Version, used by Protestants. The translation preferred by Catholics would have been the Douai Bible.]

about sixty, declared their intention not to comply with the rules of the school in that particular. And from all the evidence it was manifest that Wall was one of, if not the principal actor. He refused to repeat the Commandments for the reasons given. He was told by Mr. Mason that his father had requested him to make him repeat them, and that if he did not, to punish him severely. Wall, still refusing, was punished by the defendant with a rattan stick some three feet in length and three-eighths of an inch thick, by whipping upon his hands. From the time when the punishment commenced to the time when it ended repeated inquiries were made of Wall if he would comply with the requirements of the school. Some thirty minutes' time was occupied in the whole. During this time there were several intervals at two of which the defendant was absent from the room some little time. The blows were not given in quick succession, but with deliberation. During the chastisement Wall was encouraged by others, who told him not to give up. This was while defendant was absent from the room. The master ceased to punish when Wall submitted to the requirements of the school.

Liberty of Conscience or Insubordination?

The Bible has long been in our common schools. It was placed there by our fathers, not for the purpose of teaching sectarian religion, but a knowledge of God and of his will, whose practice is religion. It was placed there as the book best adapted from which to "teach children and youth the principles of piety, justice, and a sacred regard to truth, love to their country, humanity, and a universal benevolence, sobriety, moderation and temperance, and those other virtues which are the ornaments of human society, and the basis upon which a republican constitution is founded."

But in doing this, no scholar is requested to believe it, none to receive it as the only true version of the laws of God. The teacher enters into no argument to prove its correctness and gives no instructions in theology from it. To read the Bible in school for these and like purposes, or to require it to be read without sectarian explanations, is no interference with religious liberty.

If the plea of conscience is good against the reading or use of the Bible, why is it not equally good against any other book, or the language in which the book may be printed? . . .

The mind and the will of Wall had been prepared for insubordination and revolt by his father and the priest. His refusal to obey the commands of the school was deliberate. His offence became the more aggravated by reason of many others acting in concert with him, to put down the authority of the school. . . .

He was punished for insubordination and a determination to stand out against the lawful commands of the school. Every blow given was for a continued resistance and a new offence. The offence and the punishment went hand in hand together. The punishment ceased when the offence ceased. . . .

The defendant is discharged.

7. The Conversion of the Jews[1]

✤ Isaac M. Wise

The time will come, evangelicals averred, when Jesus Christ will reign supreme over all the earth. Before that time, not only must the heathen be converted but the Jews as well. But a people which had maintained its sense of identity despite exile, dispersion, and the ghetto, was not likely to lose it in the open society of the New World. A determination to resist assimilation may be seen in the following episode from the life of Rabbi Isaac M. Wise (1819–1900), who became the leading figure in the liberal wing of Judaism known as Reform Judaism. ∎

In December, 1847, an occurrence took place which gave me an opportunity of putting my English studies to practical use. The conversionist craze of American orthodox Christianity is well known. It was more acute here at that time than even in England or Prussia. The English Society for the Conversion of the Jews had its agents in all parts of this country, and was supported by a number of American organizations and by every Protestant clergyman. Every pious member of the Church, man or woman, was a missionary. The pursuit of souls, although unsuccessful, was yet humiliating for the Jews and Judaism. It was particularly distasteful to me, because the plan of campaign of those pietists consisted chiefly in arousing and fomenting a sentiment of pity for the poor, persecuted, and blinded Jews. . . .

[1] Isaac M. Wise, *Reminiscences* (Cincinnati: L. Wise & Co., 1901), pp. 62–68.

There was in Albany a tall, thin, smoothly-shaven, quite ignorant, very pious city missionary, whom we . . . drove into such narrow straits occasionally, that he became a quite well-behaved gentleman. He devoted his attention exclusively to sailors, corner-loafers, ne'er-do-wells, and rowdies, and let the remaining non-Christians, including the Jews, roam about unconverted. A German Methodist preacher, who had been a shoemaker, took up the conversion business also, but without success. His occupation was with feet; when it came to heads, he was unable to accomplish anything. He retired humbled from the field. A long-necked, narrow-chested schoolmistress furnished us with tracts and other pietistic writings, until she learned to her sorrow that the Jews read no English, and used the sacred tracts for wrapping-paper.

A Public Encounter

Thus far everything proceeded well in this field. One day a prominent Christian woman asked me with ill-concealed mockery, "Will you speak tonight at the great meeting?"

"At which meeting, madam?"

"In Dr. Wykoff's church," said she, smiling maliciously; "here is the notice in the *Argus*." She showed me the invitation, printed in the newspaper mentioned:

"The Rev. Rabbi Cohn, from Jerusalem, a missionary of the London Society for the improvement of the condition of the Jews, will speak this evening in Dr. Wykoff's church, with the purpose of forming a branch organization for this holy and humane work. The lower floor will be reserved exclusively for the clergy, the church officers, and their ladies. The general public will be accommodated with seats in the gallery." This was the notice. I read it, and said to the lady, "Yes, I shall speak." "And I shall listen," said she; "and my husband also." This man was the future Senator Harris.

I went home, donned my frock coat, let my wife put collar and white neckerchief on me to her great surprise, and at seven o'clock promptly I stood at the entrance of the church. The sexton wished to prevent my entering the lower floor. "Are you a Protestant clergyman?" he asked. "I am a clergyman, you know that full well, who protests against you all; consequently I am a protestant clergyman," I answered, and before he knew it I had entered the lower floor. He was compelled to leave me undisturbed, or else to have me removed by the police. He wisely chose the former alternative. I took a seat near the pulpit, and when the two Unitarian and the Universalist ministers entered, we came to the understanding that they would second anything that I would propose, and I, for my part, promised the same. The pious men and women came in large numbers. They eyed us askance. The church was entirely filled. Dr. Wykoff, in company with other prominent personages, entered at eight o'clock. A little, dark, well-fed man, with small, black eyes and a suspiciously large nose, walked in with them. The proceedings opened with prayer and song. Thereupon someone arose and moved that the meeting organize itself, with Dr. Wykoff as chairman. This was carried. Wykoff now noticed me sitting opposite the pulpit. He had to explain the object of the meeting. He coughs and stammers, and somehow or other he cannot do it successfully, for he and I were friends. At last, however, the words were out, and the unfortunate Jew was spoken of pityingly in the usual stock phrases. He finished and said, "Does anyone wish to speak on the subject?" The intention was to introduce the missionary at this point, who was to speak his piece; but I anticipated him. "I ask for the floor, Mr. Chairman." Wykoff made a wry face; but he could not refuse me the floor. Nor did I wait for his decision, but began to speak at once. It was the first time that the voice of a Jew had been heard on this question, and I could count with assurance on the undivided attention of the public. I surrendered myself completely to my emotions. I analyzed the subject thoroughly from the moral standpoint. I chastised the covetous affectation and the hypocritical sympathy of piety with all the powers at my command. I refused determinedly, in the name of the Jews, all monetary support, because we ourselves provide for our poor, our widows, and orphans, etc., and rear our children. There are no rowdies, streetwalkers, and gamblers among us. We need no help, and accept none. I had determined to treat the subject also from the theological standpoint; but the repeated applause from the gallery convinced me that this was not necessary. I contented myself with stating that I was prepared to prove that the Jew could be converted to Christianity neither by gold nor cunning, neither by persecution nor force, but that I considered it unnecessary to do so at any length at present. I then moved that the meeting adjourn *sine die*. The Unitarian minister arose with solemn mien, and seconded my motion.

The chairman could not do otherwise than put the motion, "All those in favor of adjournment will say aye." A rousing aye thundered from the gallery. "All those opposed will say no." Outside of a few women, no one had the courage to say no. The men recognized how the public in the gallery felt. Wykoff, happy to be released from his uncomfortable predicament, declared the meeting adjourned. The play was over, the audience went home, their faces a yard long. No similar meeting ever again took place in Albany, and whenever a missionary did come to town, Dr. Wykoff brought him to me, that I might explain matters to him. Then he sent him away in peace.

8. A Seneca Chief Replies to a Missionary[1]

✤ Chief Red-Jacket

Sometimes Indians were converted to Christianity by missionaries, at least superficially. But on one occasion in 1805, a Seneca chief, known to the whites as Red-Jacket, seems to have had the best of the encounter. The following translation from the Seneca tongue was widely circulated at the time, and has been several times reprinted. ■

"FRIEND AND BROTHER: It was the will of the Great Spirit that we should meet together this day. He orders all things, and has given us a fine day for our council. He has taken his garment from before the sun, and caused it to shine with brightness upon us. Our eyes are opened, that we see clearly; our ears are unstopped, that we have been able to hear distinctly the words you have spoken. For all these favors we thank the Great Spirit, and him only.

"BROTHER: This council fire was kindled by you. It was at your request that we came together at this time. We have listened with attention to what you have said. You requested us to speak our minds freely. This gives us great joy; for we now consider that we stand upright before you, and can speak what we think. All have heard your voice, and all speak to you now as one man. Our minds are agreed.

---

[1] William L. Stone, *The Life and Times of Red-Jacket, or Sa-Go-Ye-Wat-Ha* (New York: Wiley and Putnam, 1841), pp. 189–193.

"BROTHER: You say you want an answer to your talk before you leave this place. It is right you should have one, as you are a great distance from home, and we do not wish to detain you. But we will first look back a little, and tell you what our fathers have told us, and what we have heard from the white people.

"BROTHER: Listen to what we say. There was a time when our forefathers owned this great island. Their seats extended from the rising to the setting sun. The Great Spirit had made it for the use of Indians. He had created the buffalo, the deer, and other animals for food. He had made the bear and the beaver. Their skins served us for clothing. He had scattered them over the country, and taught us how to take them. He had caused the earth to produce corn for bread. All this he had done for his red children, because he loved them. If we had some disputes about our hunting ground, they were generally settled without the shedding of much blood. But an evil day came upon us. Your forefathers crossed the great water and landed on this island. Their numbers were small. They found friends and not enemies. They told us they had fled from their own country for fear of wicked men, and had come here to enjoy their religion. They asked for a small seat. We took pity on them, granted their request; and they sat down amongst us. We gave them corn and meat; they gave us poison[2] in return.

"The white people, Brother, had now found our country. Tidings were carried back, and more came amongst us. Yet we did not fear them. We took them to be friends. They called us brothers. We believed them and gave them a larger seat. At length their numbers had greatly increased. They wanted more land; they wanted our country. Our eyes were opened, and our minds became uneasy. Wars took place. Indians were hired to fight against Indians, and many of our people were destroyed. They also brought strong liquor amongst us. It was strong and powerful, and has slain thousands.

"BROTHER: Our seats were once large and yours were small. You have now become a great people, and we have scarcely a place left to spread our blankets. You have got our country, but are not satisfied; you want to force your religion upon us.

"BROTHER: Continue to listen. You say that you are sent to instruct us how to worship the Great Spirit agreeably to his mind, and, if we do not take hold of the religion which you white people teach,

---

[2] **poison:** presumably rum or whiskey.

we shall be unhappy hereafter. You say that you are right and we are lost. How do we know this to be true? We understand that your religion is written in a book. If it was intended for us as well as you, why has not the Great Spirit given to us, and not only to us, but why did he not give to our forefathers, the knowledge of that book, with the means of understanding it rightly? We only know what you tell us about it. How shall we know when to believe, being so often deceived by the white people?

"BROTHER: You say there is but one way to worship and serve the Great Spirit. If there is but one religion, why do you white people differ so much about it? Why not all agreed, as you can all read the book?

"BROTHER: We do not understand these things. We are told that your religion was given to your forefathers, and has been handed down from father to son. We also have a religion, which was given to our forefathers, and has been handed down to us their children. We worship in that way. It teaches us to be thankful for all the favors we receive, to love each other, and to be united. We never quarrel about religion.

"BROTHER: The Great Spirit has made us all, but he has made a great difference between his white and red children. He has given us different complexions and different customs. To you he has given the arts. To these he has not opened our eyes. We know these things to be true. Since he has made so great a difference between us in other things, why may we not conclude that he has given us a different religion according to our understanding? The Great Spirit does right. He knows what is best for his children; we are satisfied.

"BROTHER: We do not wish to destroy your religion, or take it from you. We only want to enjoy our own. . . .

"BROTHER: We are told that you have been preaching to the white people in this place. These people are our neighbors. We are acquainted with them. We will wait a little while, and see what effect your preaching has upon them. If we find it does them good, makes them honest and less disposed to cheat Indians, we will then consider again of what you have said.

"BROTHER: You have now heard our answer to your talk, and this is all we have to say at present. As we are going to part, we will come and take you by the hand, and hope the Great Spirit will protect you on your journey, and return you safe to your friends."

VII. Religion and the Institution of Slavery

There was a time, in the years immediately following the Revolution, when many Americans thought it plausible to suppose that the institution of slavery was gradually dying out and would disappear in the course of time. Instead it grew stronger, as cotton culture expanded across the deep South. Soon the new nation was confronted with a renewed challenge to the system of values proclaimed in the Declaration of Independence. The selections that follow show how representatives of various religious groups — black and white, slave and free, North and South — sought to come to terms with this challenge. ■

1. Go Down, Moses
✤ Traditional Spiritual

Many people in many times and places have found in the Bible words with which to articulate their own experience. It has been a mirror in which they discovered themselves. With special poignancy, slaves in the Old South expressed their longings for freedom by means of words and images drawn from the story of the bondage in Egypt. ■

When Israel was in Egypt's land,
　　Let my people go;
Oppressed so hard they could not stand,
　　Let my people go;

Refrain:
　　"Go down, Moses, 'way down in Egypt's land;

"Tell old Pharaoh
"Let my people go."

"Thus saith the Lord," bold Moses said,
   "Let my people go;
"If not I'll smite your first-born dead,
   "Let my people go."

"No more shall they in bondage toil,
   "Let my people go;
"Let them come out with Egypt's spoil,
   "Let my people go."

The Lord told Moses what to do,
   Let my people go;
To lead the children of Israel through,
   Let my people go.

When they had reached to other shore,
   Let my people go;
They sang a song of triumph o'er,
   Let my people go.

Refrain:
   "Go down, Moses, 'way down in Egypt's land;
   "Tell old Pharaoh
   "Let my people go."

2. Beginnings of the Negro Church[1]
♣ Richard Allen

A refusal on the part of Negro worshippers to accept inferior status in a predominantly white church led to the organization of an independent church and eventually a new denomination, the African Methodist Episcopal Church. The story is told by Richard Allen, the founder and first bishop of the new church.

[1] *The Life, Experience, and Gospel Labors of the Rt. Rev. Richard Allen* (Nashville, Tenn.: Abingdon Press, 1960), pp. 23–26.

*Born a slave in 1760, he was converted under Methodist in-
fluences, later obtained his freedom from his master, and became
a preacher of marked power and ability.* ■

February, 1786, I came to Philadelphia. Preaching was given out
for me at five o'clock in the morning at St. George's Church. I strove
to preach as well as I could, but it was a great cross to me; but the
Lord was with me. We had a good time and several souls were
awakened and were earnestly seeking redemption in the blood of
Christ. I thought I would stop in Philadelphia a week or two. I
preached at different places in the city. My labor was much blessed.
I soon saw a large field open in seeking and instructing my African
brethren, who had been a long forgotten people and few of them
attended public worship. . . . I saw the necessity of erecting a place of
worship for the colored people. I proposed it to the most respectable
people of color in this city; but here I met with opposition. I had but
three colored brethren that united with me in erecting a place of
worship. . . .

We all belonged to St. George's Church — Rev. Absalom Jones,
William White and Dorus Ginnings. We felt ourselves much
cramped, but my dear Lord was with us, and we believed, if it was his
will, the work would go on, and that we would be able to succeed in
building the house of the Lord. We established prayer meetings and
meetings of exhortation, and the Lord blessed our endeavors, and
many souls were awakened; but the elder soon forbade our holding
any such meetings; but we viewed the forlorn state of our colored
brethren, and that they were destitute of a place of worship. They
were considered as a nuisance.

Departure from the White Church

A number of us usually attended St. George's Church in Fourth
Street; and when the colored people began to get numerous in attending the church, they moved us from the seats we usually sat on, and
placed us around the wall, and on Sabbath morning we went to
church and the sexton stood at the door and told us to go in the
gallery. He told us to go, and we would see where to sit. We expected to take the seats over the ones we formerly occupied below, not
knowing any better. We took those seats. Meeting had begun, and
they were nearly done singing, and just as we got to the seats, the elder

said, "Let us pray." We had not been long upon our knees before I heard considerable scuffling and low talking. I raised my head up and saw one of the trustees, H— M—, having hold of the Rev. Absalom Jones, pulling him up off of his knees and saying, "You must get up — you must not kneel here." Mr. Jones replied, "Wait until prayer is over." Mr. H— M— said, "No, you must get up now or I will call for aid and force you away." Mr. Jones said, "Wait until prayer is over, and I will get up and trouble you no more." With that he beckoned to one of the other trustees, Mr. L— S— to come to his assistance. He came, and went to William White to pull him up. By this time prayer was over, and we all went out of the church in a body, and they were no more plagued with us in the church. This raised a great excitement and inquiry among the citizens, in so much that I believe they were ashamed of their conduct. But my dear Lord was with us, and we were filled with fresh vigor to get a house erected to worship God in. Seeing our forlorn and distressed situation, many of the hearts of our citizens were moved to urge us forward; notwithstanding we had subscribed largely towards finishing St. George's Church, in building the gallery and laying new floors, and just as the house was made comfortable, we were turned out from enjoying the comforts of worshiping therein. We then hired a storeroom, and held worship by ourselves. Here we were pursued with threats of being disowned, and read publicly out of meeting if we did continue worship in the place we had hired; but we believed the Lord would be our friend. We got subscription papers out to raise money to build the house of the Lord. By this time we had waited on Dr. Rush[2] and Mr. Robert Ralston, and told them of our distressing situation. We considered it a blessing that the Lord had put it into our hearts to wait upon these gentlemen. They pitied our situation, and subscribed largely towards the church, and were very friendly towards us, and advised us how to go on. We appointed Mr. Ralston our treasurer. Dr. Rush did much for us in public by his influence. I hope the name of Dr. Benjamin Rush and Robert Ralston will never be forgotten among us. They were the first two gentlemen who espoused the cause of the oppressed, and aided us in building the house of the Lord for the poor Africans to worship in. Here was the beginning and rise of the first African church in America.

[2] [**Dr. Rush:** Benjamin Rush, as well as being one of the most important pioneers in American medicine, was a signer of the Declaration of Independence and an author of an antislavery pamphlet.]

3. Black Religion in the Cotton Kingdom[1]

✤ Frederick Law Olmsted

A Northerner, critical of slavery but not an extreme abolitionist, Frederick Law Olmsted traveled through the South in 1853 and 1854 in order to learn from first-hand investigation what the economic and social effects of slavery were. His descriptions of Southern institutions and customs were vividly but honestly done, and the books compiled from his newspaper reports have become classics of American travel literature. Olmsted later became widely known as a landscape architect, responsible for the design of Central Park in New York and many other public and private projects. ■

On a Rice Plantation in Georgia

On most of the large rice plantations which I have seen in this vicinity, there is a small chapel, which the Negroes call their prayer house. The owner of one of these told me that, having furnished the prayer house with seats having a back-rail, his Negroes petitioned him to remove it, because it did not leave them room enough to pray. It was explained to me that it is their custom, in social worship, to work themselves up to a great pitch of excitement, in which they yell and cry aloud and finally shriek and leap up, clapping their hands and dancing, as it is done at heathen festivals. The back-rail they found to seriously impede this exercise.

Mr. X. told me that he had endeavoured with but little success to prevent this shouting and jumping of the Negroes at their meeting on his plantation, from a conviction that there was not the slightest element of religious sentiment in it. He considered it to be engaged in more as an exciting amusement than from any really religious impulse. In the town churches, except, perhaps, those managed and conducted almost exclusively by Negroes, the slaves are said to commonly engage in religious exercises in a sober and decorous manner; yet a member of a Presbyterian church in a Southern city told me that he had seen the Negroes in his own house of worship, during "a season of revival," leap from their seats, throw

---

[1] Frederick Law Olmsted, *The Cotton Kingdom* (New York: Mason Brothers, 1861), Vol. I, pp. 259–260, 308–313.

their arms wildly in the air, shout vehemently and unintelligibly, cry, groan, rend their clothes, and fall into cataleptic trances.

On almost every large plantation, and in every neighborhood of small ones, there is one man who has come to be considered the head or pastor of the local church. The office among the Negroes, as among all other people, confers a certain importance and power. A part of the reverence attaching to the duties is given to the person; vanity and self-confidence are cultivated, and a higher ambition aroused than can usually enter the mind of a slave. The self-respect of the preacher is also often increased by the consideration in which he is held by his master, as well as by his fellows; thus the preachers generally have an air of superiority to other Negroes; they acquire a remarkable memory of words, phrases, and forms; a curious sort of poetic talent is developed, and a habit is obtained of rhapsodizing and exciting furious emotions, to a great degree spurious and temporary, in themselves and others, through the imagination.

Sunday Morning in New Orleans

Walking this morning through a rather mean neighbourhood I was attracted by a loud chorus singing, to the open door of a chapel or small church. I found a large congregation of Negroes assembled within, and the singing being just then concluded and a Negro preacher commencing a sermon, I entered an empty pew near the entrance. I had no sooner taken a seat than a Negro usher came to me, and, in the most polite manner, whispered:

"Won't you please to let me give you a seat higher up, master, 'long o' tudder white folks?"

I followed him to the uppermost seat facing the pulpit, where there were three other white persons. One of them was a woman — old, very plain, and not as well dressed as many of the Negroes; another looked like a ship's officer, and was probably a member of the police force in undress [civilian clothes] — what we call a spy when we detect it in Europe. Both of these remained diligently and gravely attentive during the service. The third was a foreign-looking person, very flashily dressed and sporting a yellow-headed walking stick and much cheap jewelry.

The remainder of the congregation consisted entirely of colored persons, many of them, however, with light hair and hardly any perceptible indications of having African blood. On the step of the chancel were a number of children, and among these one of the loveliest young girls that I ever saw. She was a light mulatto and had an expression of unusual intelligence and vivacity. During the service she frequently smiled, I thought derisively, at the emotions and excitement betrayed by the older people about her. She was elegantly dressed, and was accompanied by a younger sister who was also dressed expensively and in good taste, but who was a shade darker, though much removed from the blackness of the true Negro, and of very good features and pleasant expression.

The preacher was nearly black, with close woolly hair. His figure was slight, he seemed to be about thirty years of age, and the expression of his face indicated a refined and delicately sensitive nature. His eye was very fine, bright, deep, and clear; his voice and manner generally quiet and impressive. . . .

As soon as I had taken my seat, my attention was attracted by an old Negro near me, whom I supposed for some time to be suffering under some nervous complaint. He trembled, his teeth chattered, and his face, at intervals, was convulsed. He soon began to respond aloud to the sentiments of the preacher, in such words as these: "Oh, yes!" "That's it, that's it!" "Yes, yes — glory — yes" and similar expressions could be heard from all parts of the house whenever the speaker's voice was unusually solemn or his language and manner eloquent or excited.

Sometimes the outcries and responses were not confined to ejaculations of this kind, but shouts and groans, terrific shrieks, and indescribable expressions of ecstasy — of pleasure or agony — and even stamping, jumping, and clapping of hands were added. The tumult often resembled that of an excited political meeting, and I was once surprised to find my own muscles all stretched as if ready for a struggle — my face glowing and my feet stamping — having been infected unconsciously, as men often are, with instinctive bodily sympathy with the excitement of the crowd. So wholly unintellectual was the basis of this excitement, however, that I could not, when my mind retroverted to itself, find any connection or meaning in the phrases of the speaker that remained in my memory; and I have no doubt it was his "action" rather than his sentiments that had given rise to the excitement of the congregation.

The Dance as an Expression of Religious Fervor

The preacher was drawing his sermon to a close and offering some sensible and pertinent advice soberly and calmly, and the congregation was attentive and comparatively quiet, when a small old woman, perfectly black, among those in the gallery, suddenly rose and began dancing and clapping her hands, at first with a slow and measured movement, and then with increasing rapidity, at the same time beginning to shout, "ha ha!" The women about her arose also, and tried to hold her, as there appeared great danger that she would fall out of the gallery, and those below left their pews that she might not fall upon them.

The preacher continued his remarks — much the best part of his sermon — but it was plain that they were wasted; every one was looking at the dancing woman in the gallery, and many were shouting and laughing aloud (in joyful sympathy, I suppose). His eye flashed as he glanced anxiously from the woman to the people, and then stopping in the middle of a sentence, a sad smile came over his face; he closed the book and bowed his head upon his hands to the desk. A voice in the congregation struck into a tune, and the whole congregation rose and joined in a roaring song. The woman was still shouting and dancing, her head thrown back and rolling from one side to the other. Gradually her shout became indistinct, she threw her arms wildly about instead of clapping her hands, fell back into the arms of her companions, then threw herself forward and embraced those before her, then tossed herself from side to side, gasping, and finally sank to the floor, where she remained at the end of the song, kicking as if acting a death struggle.

4. Slavery Defended on Scriptural Grounds[1]

✤ *James Henry Hammond*

The authority of Scripture was so much taken for granted by Americans that proslavery and antislavery pamphleteers alike turned to it to buttress their respective positions. The author of

[1] James Henry Hammond, "Slavery in the Light of Political Science," in E. N. Elliott, ed., *Cotton is King, and Pro-Slavery Arguments* (Augusta, Ga.: Pritchard, Abbott & Loomis, 1860), pp. 634–636.

the selection that follows was governor of South Carolina, United States senator, a leading states-rights advocate, and an extremist among defenders of slavery and critics of the abolitionists. ■

The Old Testament Argument

Let us contemplate [slavery] as it is. And thus contemplating it, the first question we have to ask ourselves is whether it is contrary to the will of God as revealed to us in his Holy Scriptures — the only certain means given us to ascertain his will. If it is, then slavery is a sin. . . .

Let us open these Holy Scriptures. In the twentieth chapter of Exodus, seventeenth verse, I find the following words: "Thou shalt not covet thy neighbor's house, thou shalt not covet thy neighbor's wife, nor his manservant, nor his maidservant, nor his ox, nor his ass, nor any thing that is thy neighbor's" — which is the tenth of those Commandments that declare the essential principles of the great moral law delivered to Moses by God himself. Now discarding all technical and verbal quibbling as wholly unworthy to be used in interpreting the word of God, what is the plain meaning, undoubted intent, and true spirit of this Commandment? Does it not emphatically and explicitly forbid you to disturb your neighbor in the enjoyment of his property; and more especially of that which is here specifically mentioned as being lawfully, and by this commandment made sacredly his? Prominent in the catalogue stands his "manservant and his maidservant," who are thus distinctly *consecrated as his property*, and guaranteed to him for his exclusive benefit, in the most solemn manner. . . . The real question, then, is what idea is intended to be conveyed by the words used in the commandment quoted? And it is clear to my mind, that as no limitation is affixed to them, and the express intention was to secure to mankind the peaceful enjoyment of every species of property, that the terms "menservants and maidservants" include all classes of servants, and establish a lawful, exclusive, and indefeasible interest equally in the "Hebrew brother who shall go out in the seventh year" and "the yearly hired servant" and "those purchased from the heathen round about" who were to be "bondmen forever" *as the property of their fellow-man*.

You cannot deny that there were among the Hebrews "bondmen forever." You cannot deny that God especially authorized his chosen people to purchase "bondmen forever" from the heathen, as recorded in the twenty-fifth chapter of Leviticus, and that they are there designated by the very Hebrew word used in the Tenth Commandment. Nor can you deny that a "bondman forever" is a "slave."...

Slavery Sanctioned by Christ and His Apostles

Although slavery in its most revolting form was everywhere visible around them, no visionary notions of piety or philanthropy ever tempted them to gainsay the law, even to mitigate the cruel severity of the existing system. On the contrary, regarding slavery as an *established,* as well as *inevitable condition of human society,* they never hinted at such a thing as its termination on earth, any more than that "the poor may cease out of the land," which God affirms to Moses shall never be. . . . St. Paul actually apprehended a runaway slave and sent him to his master! Instead of deriving from the gospel any sanction for the work you have undertaken, it would be difficult to imagine sentiments and conduct more strikingly in contrast than those of the Apostles and the abolitionists.

It is impossible, therefore, to suppose that slavery is contrary to the will of God. It is equally absurd to say that American slavery differs in form or principle from that of the chosen people. *We accept the Bible terms as the definition of our slavery, and its precepts as the guide of our conduct.* . . .

I think, then, I may safely conclude, and I firmly believe, that American slavery is not only not a sin, but especially commanded by God through Moses and approved by Christ through his Apostles. And here I might close its defense; for what God ordains and Christ sanctifies should surely command the respect and toleration of man.

BEGINNINGS OF THE NEGRO CHURCH: *Rev. Richard Allen (left), a freed slave, organized the African Methodist Episcopal Church in Philadelphia in the late eighteenth century.*

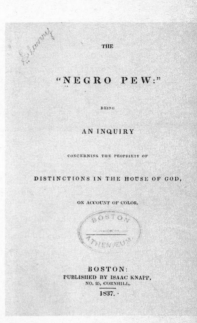

THE

"NEGRO PEW:"

BEING

AN INQUIRY

CONCERNING THE PROPRIETY OF

DISTINCTIONS IN THE HOUSE OF GOD,

ON ACCOUNT OF COLOR.

BOSTON
ATHENÆUM

BOSTON:
PUBLISHED BY ISAAC KNAPP,
NO. 25, CORNHILL.
1837.

Provocation for starting a separate church was the inferior status to which Negroes had been relegated in most white churches. One evidence of this was the "Negro pew" — the subject of the treatise pictured at right.

Services in the Negro churches reflected both the needs and experiences of black people. Release from oppression was a recurring theme in their music and worship. Contemporary white chroniclers were struck with the religious fervor displayed in many Negro churches, typified in the scene below.

5. An Antislavery Revival Meeting[1]

❖ Henry B. Stanton

*The relationships between religion and the antislavery move-
ment were many and various. Often antislavery writers used
biblical and theological arguments. Sometimes the intensity of
their commitment to the cause of abolitionism was religious in
character, and their antislavery societies became, for them, sub-
stitutes for the churches. The way of organizing antislavery
societies was similar to that used by missionary and Bible
societies. In 1834, the students of Lane Theological Seminary in
Cincinnati discussed slavery for eighteen consecutive evenings,
just as though they were running one of Finney's revivals. By the
time this antislavery "protracted meeting" was over, almost everyone had been converted.* ■

Slavery and its proposed remedies — immediate abolition and
colonization — have been subjects of occasional remark among the
students since the commencement of the late term (June). A flour-
ishing Colonization Society[2] has existed among us almost from the
foundation of the institution. Our interest in these topics increased
gradually until about the first of February, when it was resolved that
we discuss publicly the merits of the colonization and abolition
schemes. At this time there were but few decided abolitionists in the
seminary. The two following questions were discussed separately:

1st. "Ought the people of the slaveholding states to abolish slavery
immediately?"

2d. "Are the doctrines, tendencies, and measures of the American
Colonization Society and the influence of its principal supporters such
as render it worthy of the patronage of the Christian public?"

Our respected faculty, fearing the effect the discussion would have
upon the prosperity of the seminary, formally advised that it should
be postponed indefinitely. But the students, feeling great anxiety that
it should proceed, and being persuaded from the state of feeling

---

[1] [Henry B. Stanton], *Debate at the Lane Seminary, Cincinnati* (Boston:
Garrison and Knapp, 1834), pp. 3–7.

[2] [**Colonization Society:** Supporters of colonization argued that the way to
solve the problem of slavery was to return free Negroes to Africa.]

among them that it would be conducted in a manner becoming young men looking forward to the ministry of the gospel of reconciliation, resolved to go on. The president and the members of the faculty, with one exception, were present during parts of the discussion.

Each question was debated nine evenings of two hours and a half each, making forty-five hours of solid debate.

Evils of Slavery Reviewed

The first speaker occupied nearly two evenings in presenting facts concerning slavery and immediate emancipation, gathered from various authentic documents. Conclusions and inferences were then drawn from these facts, and arguments founded upon them favorable to immediate abolition, during the two next evenings. Nearly four of the remaining five evenings were devoted to the recital of facts in regard to slavery, slaves, and slaveholders, gathered, not from written documents, but from careful personal observation and experience. Nearly half of the seventeen speakers on the evenings last alluded to were the sons of slaveholders; one had been a slaveholder himself; one had till recently been a slave; and the residue were residents of, or had recently travelled or lived in, slave states. From their testimony the following facts and premises were established, to wit: That slaves long for freedom; that it is a subject of very frequent conversation among them; that they know their masters have no right to hold them in slavery; that they keenly feel the wrong, the insult, and the degradation which are heaped upon them by the whites. They feel no interest comparatively in their master's affairs because they know he is their oppressor. They are indolent, because nothing they can earn is their own. They pretend to be more ignorant and stupid than they really are, so as to avoid responsibility and to shun the lash for any real or alleged disobedience to orders. When inspired with a promise of freedom, they will toil with incredible alacrity and faithfulness. They tell their masters and drivers they are contented with their lot merely through fear of greater cruelty if they tell the truth. No matter how kind their master is, they are dissatisfied, and would rather be his hired servants than his slaves. The slave drivers are generally low, brutal, debauched men, distinguished only for their cruelty and licentiousness; they generally have the despotic control of the slaves. The best side of slavery is seen, its darker features being known only to slaves, masters and drivers. (Upon this point, horrid facts in regard to the whipping and murdering of slaves were developed. God sparing my life, they shall be given to the public.) The state of morals among slaves, especially in regard to licentiousness, is sickening! This condition is attributable to the treatment they receive from their masters, they being huddled together from their infancy in small apartments without discrimination of sex, and oftentimes being compelled to steal or starve. The influence of slavery upon the physical condition and mental and moral character of the whites is decidedly and lamentably pernicious. The internal slave trade is increasing and is carried on by men distinguished even among slave drivers for their cruelty and brutality.

Testimony of an Ex-Slave

James Bradley, the emancipated slave, . . . addressed us nearly two hours, and I wish his speech could have been heard by every opponent of immediate emancipation, to wit: first, that "it would be unsafe to the community;" second, that "the condition of the emancipated Negroes would be worse than it now is; that they are incompetent to provide for themselves; that they would become paupers and vagrants, and would rather steal than work for wages." This shrewd and intelligent black cut up these white objections by the roots, and withered and scorched them under the sun of sarcastic argumentation for nearly an hour, to which the assembly responded in repeated and spontaneous roars of laughter, which were heartily joined in by both colonizationists and abolitionists. Do not understand me as saying, that his speech was devoid of argument. No. It contained sound logic, enforced by apt illustrations. I wish the slanderers of Negro intellect could have witnessed this unpremeditated effort. . . .

At the close of the ninth evening the vote was taken on the first question, *when every individual voted in the affirmative except four or five*, who excused themselves from voting at all on the ground that they had not made up their opinion. Every friend of the cause rendered a hearty tribute of thanksgiving to God for the glorious issue.

Colonization Rejected

At the next evening we entered upon the discussion of the second question. Here there was a much greater diversity of sentiment. But we entered upon the debate not like blinded partisans, but like men whose polar star was facts and truth, whose needle was conscience, whose chart the Bible.

The witnesses summoned to the stand were the documents of the Colonization Society. They were examined at great length and in great numbers. We judged it out of its own mouth. There was no paucity of testimony; for, as I before observed, we had all its "repositories," and nearly all its reports and addresses, in addition to which we were benevolently furnished by friends with numerous collated witnesses whom we of course had the privilege of cross-examining. Notwithstanding the length of this part of the discussion, but two individuals spoke, one on each side, and another read some testimony in favor of the colony. Several individuals at the opening of the debate intended to speak on the affirmative, but before it was closed they became warmly attached to the other side. Others were induced to espouse the cause of anticolonizationism by examining documents of the Colonization Society for the purpose of preparing to speak in the affirmative. Most of the colonizationists who expressed any opinion on the subject declared their ignorance of the doctrines and measures of the [Colonization] Society until this debate. They cannot find words to express their astonishment that they should have been so duped into the support of this society as a scheme of benevolence toward the free blacks and a remedy for slavery. They now repudiate it with all their hearts. . . .

At the close of the debate the question was taken by ayes and noes, and decided in the negative with only one dissenting voice. Four or five who did not regularly attend the discussion declined voting. Two or three others were absent from the seminary. When the debate commenced I had fears that there might be some unpleasant excitement, particularly as slaveholders and prospective heirs to slave property were to participate in it. But the kindest feelings prevailed. There was no crimination, no denunciation, no impeachment of motives. And the result has convinced me that prejudice is vincible, that colonization is vulnerable, and that immediate emancipation is not only right and practicable, but is "expedient." . . .

This evening we formed an antislavery society.

6. The Civil War as an Apocalyptic Event[1]

♣ Julia Ward Howe

When Julia Ward Howe sought new words for the tune of "John Brown's Body," the images that flooded her mind were ones that millennial preaching had made widely familiar. They were drawn from the Biblical book of the Revelation of John, also known as the Apocalypse. The coming of the Lord, the grapes of wrath, the terrible swift sword, the sifting of the hearts of men on the Day of Judgment — all these are reminders of the extent to which the second coming and millennial reign of Christ, and the Last Judgment, had become part of the American consciousness. And so, in the crisis of the Civil War, understood as an apocalyptic event, Mrs. Howe's hymn drew resonance from the deep and mysterious sources of American faith. ■

Mine eyes have seen the glory of the coming of the Lord:
He is trampling out the vintage where the grapes of wrath are stored;
He hath loosed the fateful lightning of His terrible swift sword.
       His truth is marching on.

I have seen Him in the watch-fires of a hundred circling camps;
They have builded Him an altar in the evening dews and damps;
I can read His righteous sentence by the dim and flaring lamps;
       His day is marching on.

I have read a fiery gospel writ in burnished rows of steel:
"As ye deal with my contemners, so with you my grace shall deal;
Let the Hero, born of woman, crush the serpent with his heel,
       Since God is marching on."

He has sounded forth the trumpet that shall never call retreat;
He is sifting out the hearts of men before His judgment-seat:
Oh, be swift, my soul, to answer Him! be jubilant, my feet!
       Our God is marching on.

In the beauty of the lilies Christ was born across the sea,
With a glory in his bosom that transfigures you and me:
As he died to make men holy, let us die to make men free,
       While God is marching on.

---

[1] Julia Ward Howe, "The Battle Hymn of the Republic," *Atlantic Monthly*, IX (1862), 145.

.*Part Three*

The Evangelical Tradition at Bay

Part Three: Introduction

Evangelical Protestantism continued to be a powerful force in American life after the Civil War, but its dominant position was eroded by new developments of various kinds. Its individualistic piety, shaped by rural and small town life, seemed inadequate to grapple with the problems of large cities and large-scale industrial enterprise. The traditional understanding of the Scriptures as the revealed Word of God was confronted by new scientific concepts in biology and physics, as well as by a critical examination of the Bible itself. And the mainline Protestant churches, especially in the cities, found themselves surrounded by fresh rivals, partly because of immigration from southern and eastern Europe, and partly because of the development of new Protestant sects. ■

VIII. A New Setting: Urbanized and Industrialized America

The growth of cities and the development of big business and large-scale industry presented evangelical Protestantism with a new setting in which to work. Religious leaders responded in various ways. The great revivalists of the day tried to adapt big business methods in order to reach the urban masses. Other churchmen experimented with new kinds of churches. And spokesmen for the "social gospel" argued that the misery of the poor and outcast had to be eliminated by social reform, not palliated by individual acts of charity. ■

1. Moody's Urban Revivalism[1]

✤ George P. Fisher

With Dwight L. Moody (1837–1899), the American revivalistic tradition entered the new world of growing industry and burgeoning cities. Contemporaries often commented on Moody's skill in using business methods of organization and on his attempts to bring evangelical religion to the urban masses. Even a professor of ecclesiastical history at Yale commended him for his work. ■

Moody's Personal Qualities

His quickness of perception, his sound understanding mingled with a large element of New England shrewdness, his rare power to lead and organize and to marshal to his side efficient colaborers, are quite remarkable. . . . Day after day and week after week he comes up to his

---

[1] George P. Fisher, "Recent Evangelistic Movements," *New Englander*, N.S. Vol. II (1879), pp. 35, 39–40.

work with unabated vivacity — his eye as bright and kind, and his heart as warm as at the beginning. He has too much love in him ever to be a fanatic. One may occasionally demur to some of his statements of doctrine, or to some of his precepts respecting the Christian life. But I have no words to utter concerning Mr. Moody but those of respect and commendation. God bless him and be with him in his labors!

Reaching the Urban Masses

We may discount all that is due to mere curiosity in bringing men together to hear Mr. Moody. It remains true that multitudes of every grade of intelligence, both in this country and in Great Britain, have thronged his meetings under the impulse of a deeper feeling. This may not be a conspicuously religious era. The mind of the community is not absorbed, as at some past epochs, in religious meditations and controversies. There is a zeal for knowledge in the secular sphere. Politics and business engross the attention of many. But we may rest assured that these great themes — life, death, and immortality — have not lost their power to stir the soul. The problems of religion are still felt to be of the deepest moment. The question — "What shall I do to be saved?" — is silently asked by thousands who never make it audible; and if a preacher appears who is somehow felt to have the secret of the Gospel and to be able to help others to a satisfactory solution of this practical question, men will go to hear him. . . .

The question is brought before us: How shall the mass of the people be brought to frequent our churches?

In our large towns the rich and the poor do not worship together. Much noble Christian work is done through mission schools and chapels. But the poor and uninstructed classes, as far as they are reached by efforts of this kind, are gathered by themselves in separate assemblies.

Another fact is that a great number of the laboring class who would not be reckoned among the objects of missionary effort and who do not lack intelligence, do not feel at home in our churches. Where the pews are elegantly furnished and rented at a high price, where fine carriages stand at the door, and where the bulk of the congregation appear in showy and expensive apparel the reluctance of the class to which I refer to attend worship may be naturally accounted for. But where these circumstances do not exist to repel their attendance by the tax which that attendance would impose or by the diffidence or envy which stand in the way of it, it is still, I believe, the fact that numbers who would go to a "tabernacle" or a public hall to hear an earnest preacher cannot be enticed into a church. Explain it as we may, we are bound to take this fact into consideration in our efforts to do good. It has occurred to me that we need not confine our preaching services so closely to the houses dedicated to religious worship; that in large towns it would be well to have sermons delivered at different centers, in halls and other places of assembly, and to seek to rally the people to these meetings by giving them a character more informal and more resembling political gatherings and the lectures to which they are accustomed. The Methodist camp meeting, perhaps, in the older portions of the country, may have outlived its usefulness. But possibly we may take a hint from what has been accomplished by such meetings in the past.

2. The Institutional Church[1]

✦ Edmund K. Alden

As cities grew in size, older residential areas were often invaded by business activities or were taken over by newly-arrived immigrants. The old inhabitants moved to less congested areas further out. Usually they sold their old church buildings and built anew. But sometimes they tried to maintain a presence in the inner city by using the old buildings for radically new programs. The result was the "institutional church," of which the Berkeley Temple in Boston was a well known example. Inescapably, however, the situation was one in which "we" (upper class, middle class) organize something for "them" (working class). ∎

One of the first things which strikes an observer is the thoroughness of organization. The extent to which division of labor is pushed would gratify a pronounced bureaucrat, and the results are far more satisfactory than those visible in the case of bureaucracies. There lies

[1] Edmund K. Alden, "The Berkeley Temple of To-Day," *Christian Union*, January 9, 1892, p. 78.

before us the schedule for one of the weeks in December, 1891. In this list thirty-six exercises are mentioned. Besides the usual preaching services, Sunday-school, and prayer meetings of the church and of the Christian Endeavor Societies, there are included an assembly of the Chinese Young Men's Christian Association, the Superintendents' Union, Sunday schools for Chinese, Armenians, and Greeks, the Berkeley Temperance Union, the Berkeley Temple Total Abstinence Guild, a pastors' reception in the vestries, a Home-Workers' meeting, a Talitha-Cumi Circle, an appointment for the Brotherhood of Andrew and Philip, an English evening school, a sewing school, a kitchen garden, classes in painting, crayon drawing, mechanical drawing, stenography, dressmaking, millinery, elocution, German, penmanship, and a newspaper class. Something here, one might think, for almost every one, either in helping or in receiving help, or in both. Such a program calls for a large working staff, and such varied activities require considerable space, severely taxing the twenty-one rooms which compose the building. Good head-work has systematized these manifold fields of endeavor, from the more purely religious efforts to those which touch closely upon the business and material world.

A commendable example of beneficent organization is afforded by the Hospitality Committees. Almost every attendant at a city church knows how the good of the preaching and of the other services is too often counterbalanced by the peculiar actions of some ushers, and by the glacial Christianity of fellow-worshipers and church members. But here the stranger to the city often finds that his advent is known to the Vestibule Committee. Ushers lie in wait for visitors on their entrance into the building in order to welcome them as to a new home. Bands of "Social Workers" subdivide the auditorium into districts of four pews each, and stand ready at the close of the morning service to greet all strangers, and to introduce them to some of the church's numerous activities. Lastly, there is a Visiting Committee of ladies who supplement the pastoral work by calls on the sick, the neglected, the poor, or the simply lonesome and downhearted.

Chinese Sunday schools are not uncommon in modern times; several of these the Berkeley Temple possesses, and also a separate school for Armenians and another for Greeks. Useful among the philanthropies is the Relief Department, which carefully sifts all applications for material aid, and, in worthy cases, relieves immediate want, either alone or in connection with the Associated Charities of

Boston. The church authorities receive many requests to furnish situations; but the establishment of an employment bureau proved impracticable, and persons out of work are provided with introductions to other agencies. One very helpful phase of practical Christianity is shown in the "Country Week," which complements the labors of the other fresh-air funds; in this way many tired women, children, and invalids are enabled to enjoy country life for a few days in the hottest part of the summer.

If time permitted, we should like to do more than glance at the Yoke-Fellows' Band and the Brotherhood of Andrew and Philip, whose members devote themselves to personal, hand-to-hand, face-to-face influence with all classes — strangers, casual visitors, non-church-goers, and church members; at the Young Men's Institute, at the Kitchen Garden for little girls, at the Kindergarten, newly established, equipped, and conducted by a young lady. Then there is the Talitha-Cumi Circle — of somewhat enigmatic title — whose meetings for the enlightenment and physical, mental, and moral uplifting of girls and young women are very helpful; and the "Outing Club," which has organized many pleasant social excursions during the summer months.

Requisitions upon the managers are constantly pouring in, faster than the supply. A gymnasium is projected; a dispensary and a boys' club are looming up in the near future. But the increasing demands call for increased funds. Already there is need either of radical alterations in the church property or of the demolition of the present building and the erection of a new one with enlarged facilities for usefulness.

What are the causes of the steady development? One cause, no doubt, is the admirably planned location, closely adjoining the quarters of the poor, rich, and "that most difficult body to reach, the middle class." But advantages of situation alone would go but part way in explanation of the success. The wealth of the church is its large force of helpers, salaried and volunteer; they are picked men and women, from those who are the head and front of the enterprise, Mr. Dickinson and his assistant pastors, Messrs. Tobey and Kelsey, through the various grades of officers, commissioned and noncommissioned. With a continuance of the same spirit and with larger means, may we not expect to find the Berkeley Temple still further solving the problems that "baffle and burden the Church of Christ"?

3. Beginnings of the Social Gospel[1]

✤ Washington Gladden

If the increased urbanization of American life presented the churches with new problems, so too did its growing industrialization. Washington Gladden (1836–1918), minister of a Congregational church in Springfield, Massachusetts, was one of the first to argue that if evangelical piety continued to concentrate on the salvation of individual souls, it would fail to meet the needs of people whose day-by-day existence was determined not by what they as individuals could make of their lives, but by the decisions of the entrepreneurs who controlled large industrial enterprises and employed large numbers of workers. ■

It was about this time that I began the series of lectures to "Workingmen and their Employers," which were published in 1876 in a volume with that title. The field was one into which the pulpit had not often ventured, and my work had to be largely that of a pioneer. But it was becoming increasingly evident that a great social problem was thus forcing itself upon the thought of the world — a problem in the solution of which the Christian church must have a large concern. Primarily it must be a question of conduct, a question concerning the relations of man to man, and it is the primary business of Christianity to define and regulate these relations. The application of the Christian law to industrial society would, it seemed to me, solve this problem, and the church ought to know how to apply it.

Against this assumption strenuous objection was raised in those days, and the protest is still heard. It was said that the minister has no business to bring questions of this kind into the pulpit; that his concern is with spiritual interests, and not with secular; that his function is the saving of souls and not the regulation of business. It was urged that if men are only "saved," all questions of this nature will solve themselves; that right relations will necessarily be established between social classes.

In dealing with this objection, it was only too apparent that the facts did not support it. It was by no means true that those who in

---

[1] Washington Gladden, *Recollections* (Boston: Houghton Mifflin Co., 1909), pp. 250–254. Reprinted by permission of the Columbus School for Girls.

THE SOCIAL GOSPEL: A movement with wide repercussions for American religion began within Protestant Christianity in the last quarter of the nineteenth century. Its aim was to bring the social order into conformity with the teachings of Jesus.

Walter Rauschenbusch (right) and Washington Gladden (above), Protestant ministers of the late 1800's, were early proponents of the "social gospel".

Unafraid of speaking out on important social issues, clergy of all faiths frequently issue unified declarations on matters of common concern. Shown here are prominent religious leaders in a 1966 peace vigil before the Tomb of the Unknown Soldier. They had just demonstrated against the Vietnam war.

the judgment of charity were "saved" were establishing right relations between themselves and those with whom they were associated in industry. Many of them were practicing injustice and cruelty, without any sense of the evil of their conduct. They were nearly all assuming that the Christian rule of life had no application to business; that the law of supply and demand was the only law which, in the world of exchanges, they were bound to respect. If a man was converted and joined the church, it did not occur to him that that fact had any relation to the management of his mill or his factory. Business was business and religion was religion; the two areas were not coterminous, they might be mutually exclusive. Nothing was more needed in the church than the enforcement upon the consciences of men of the truth that the Christian law covers every relation of life, and the distinct and thoroughgoing application of that law to the common affairs of men. . . .

Let us say that our business is saving souls. Souls are men. How to save men, their manhood, their character — that is our chief problem. Is there any other realm in which character, manhood, is more rapidly and more inevitably made or lost, than this realm of industry? Is the man saved, who, in his dealings with his employee, or his employer, can habitually seek his own aggrandizement at the cost of the other? Is not the selfishness which is expected to rule in all this department of life the exact antithesis of Christian morality? Is there anything else from which men need more to be saved than from the habits of thought and action which prevail in the places where "business is business"? Are we really "saving souls" when we permit men like the packinghouse proprietors and the insurance wreckers to sit comfortably in our pews and enjoy our ministrations? I fear that some of these men may have grave accusations to bring against us, one of these days, for having failed to tell them the truth about their own conduct.

In fact, there is reason for the belief that in these very questions respecting the regulation of our industries, the Christian church is facing today its crucial test. If it can meet these questions frankly and bravely, if it can solve them successfully, its future is secure. It will have won its right to the moral leadership of society. If it fails in this, if this tremendous problem is worked out without its aid, the world is likely to have very little use for it in the generations to come. The church is in the world to save the world; if it lacks the power to do this, and industrial society plunges into chaos, are there any ecclesiastics infatuated enough to believe that the church can save itself out of that wreck? No; it must save society, or go to ruin with it.

4. Christianity and the Social Crisis[1]

✣ Walter Rauschenbusch

Of spokesmen for the Social Gospel, none has cast a longer shadow than Walter Rauschenbusch (1861–1918). He had first-hand experience with human misery while minister of a Baptist church in New York City from 1886 to 1897. He later taught at Rochester Theological Seminary. His writings on social issues were intellectually disciplined without losing a sense of the immediacy of human social problems. ∎

The social crisis offers a great opportunity for the infusion of new life and power into the religious thought of the Church. It also offers the chance for progress in its life. When the broader social outlook widens the purpose of a Christian man beyond the increase of his church, he lifts up his eyes and sees that there are others who are at work for humanity besides his denomination. Common work for social welfare is the best common ground for the various religious bodies and the best training school for practical Christian unity. The strong movement for Christian union in our country has been largely prompted by the realization of social needs, and is led by men who have felt the attraction of the kingdom of God as something greater than any denomination and as the common object of all. Thus the divisions which were caused in the past by differences in dogma and church polity may perhaps be healed by unity of interest in social salvation.

As we have seen, the industrial and commercial life today is dominated by principles antagonistic to the fundamental principles of Christianity, and it is so difficult to live a Christian life in the midst of it that few men even try. If production could be organized on a

[1] Walter Rauschenbusch, *Christianity and the Social Crisis* (New York: The Macmillan Company, 1907), pp. 340–342.

basis of co-operative fraternity, if distribution could at least approximately be determined by justice, if all men could be conscious that their labor contributed to the welfare of all and that their personal well-being was dependent on the prosperity of the commonwealth, if predatory business and parasitic wealth ceased and all men lived only by their labor, if the luxury of unearned wealth no longer made us all feverish with covetousness and a simpler life became the fashion, if our time and strength were not used up either in getting a bare living or in amassing unusable wealth and we had more leisure for the higher pursuits of the mind and the soul — then there might be a chance to live such a life of gentleness and brotherly kindness and tranquillity of heart as Jesus desired for men. It may be that the co-operative commonwealth would give us the first chance in history to live a really Christian life without retiring from the world, and would make the Sermon on the Mount a philosophy of life feasible for all who care to try.

This is the stake of the church in the social crisis. If society continues to disintegrate and decay, the church will be carried down with it. If the church can rally such moral forces that injustice will be overcome and fresh red blood will course in a sounder social organism, it will itself rise to higher liberty and life. Doing the will of God it will have new visions of God. With a new message will come a new authority. If the salt lose its saltness, it will be trodden under foot. If the church fulfills its prophetic functions, it may bear the prophet's reproach for a time, but it will have the prophet's vindication thereafter.

The conviction has always been embedded in the heart of the church that "the world" — society as it is — is evil and some time is to make way for a true human society in which the spirit of Jesus Christ shall rule. For fifteen hundred years those who desired to live a truly Christian life withdrew from the evil world to live a life apart. But the principle of such an ascetic departure from the world is dead in modern life. There are only two other possibilities. The church must either condemn the world and seek to change it, or tolerate the world and conform to it. In the latter case it surrenders its holiness and its mission. The other possibility has never yet been tried with faith on a large scale. All the leadings of God in contemporary history and all the promptings of Christ's spirit in our hearts urge us to make the trial. On this choice is staked the future of the church.

5. The Social Creed of the Churches[1]

✤ *The Federal Council of Churches*

A concern for the social application of religion was one of the chief reasons for the organization in 1905 of the Federal Council of Churches (predecessor of the present National Council of Churches), and a "Social Creed" was an early result. ■

The Federal Council of the Churches of Christ in America stands:

For equal rights and complete justice for all men in all stations of life.

For the abolition of child labor.

For such regulation of the conditions of toil for women as shall safeguard the physical and moral health of the community.

For the suppression of the "Sweating System."

For the gradual and reasonable reduction of the hours of labor to the lowest practicable point, and for that degree of leisure for all which is the condition of the highest human life.

For a release from employment one day in seven.

For the right of all men to the opportunity for self-maintenance, a right ever to be wisely and strongly safeguarded against encroachments of every kind.

For the right of workers to some protection against the hardships often resulting from the swift crises of industrial change.

For a living wage as a minimum in every industry, and for the highest wage that each industry can afford.

For the protection of the worker from dangerous machinery, occupational disease, injuries, and mortality.

For suitable provision for the old age of the workers and for those incapacitated by injury.

For the principle of conciliation and arbitration in industrial dissensions.

For the abatement of poverty.

For the most equitable division of the products of industry that can ultimately be devised.

---

[1] Harry F. Ward, *The Social Creed of the Churches* (New York: Abingdon Press, 1914), p. 6.

IX. The Enlarging Pluralism of American Religion

There was a time, in the colonial period, when religious pluralism in America meant simply a variety of Protestant groups. In the first half of the nineteenth century, it came to mean Roman Catholicism as well. By the end of the century, there were more Protestant sects than ever, Catholicism represented a larger proportion of the population, and immigration from eastern Europe had introduced significant numbers of communicants of the Eastern (or Orthodox) Churches. The number and proportion of Jews was growing rapidly also, especially because of immigration from Russia. No longer could spokesmen for evangelical Protestantism casually assume that they were the special custodians of American values and shapers of American destiny. ■

1. Mrs. Eddy's Great Discovery[1]

✤ Mary Baker G. Eddy

Christian Science likewise grew and flourished in the period after the Civil War. It rediscovered a concern for healing as part of the ministry of religion, something Protestantism, especially, had long disregarded. Thereby it seems to have met the religious needs of many whose ills were, in some degree, the result of the stresses and strains of an urban and industrial society. ■

It was in Massachusetts, in February, 1866 . . . that I discovered the Science of Divine Metaphysical Healing, which I afterwards named Christian Science. The discovery came to pass in this way. During twenty years prior to my discovery I had been trying to trace

[1] Mary Baker G. Eddy, *Retrospection and Introspection* (Boston: Joseph Armstrong, 1900), pp. 38–42.

128

all physical effects to a mental cause, and in the latter part of 1866 I gained the Scientific certainty that all causation was Mind and every effect a mental phenomenon.

My immediate recovery from the effects of an injury caused by an accident, an injury that neither medicine nor surgery could reach, was the falling apple that led me to the discovery how to be well myself and how to make others so.

Even to the . . . physician who attended me and rejoiced in my recovery, I could not then explain the *modus* [manner] of my relief. I could only assure him that the divine Spirit had wrought the miracle —a miracle which later I found to be in perfect Scientific accord with divine law.

I then withdrew from society about three years to ponder my mission, to search the Scriptures, to find the Science of Mind that should take the things of God and show them to the creature and reveal the great curative principle — Deity.

The Bible was my textbook. It answered my questions as to how I was healed; but the Scriptures had to me a new meaning, a new tongue. Their spiritual signification appeared and I apprehended for the first time in their spiritual meaning Jesus' teaching and demonstration, and the Principle and rule of spiritual Science and Metaphysical Healing — in a word, Christian Science.

I named it *Christian*, because it is compassionate, helpful, and spiritual. God I called *Immortal Mind*. That which sins, suffers, and dies I named *mortal mind*. The physical senses, or sensuous nature, I called *error* and *shadow*. Soul I denominated *Substance*, because Soul alone is truly substantial. God I characterized as individual entity, but his corporeality I denied. The Real I claimed as eternal; and its antipodes [opposites], or the temporal, I described as unreal. Spirit I called the *reality*, and matter the *unreality*.

I knew the human conception of God to be that he was a physically personal being like unto man, and that the five physical senses are so many witnesses to the physical personality of mind and the real existence of matter, but I learned that these material senses testify falsely, that matter neither sees, hears, nor feels Spirit, and is therefore inadequate to form any proper conception of the infinite Mind. "If I bear witness of myself my witness is not true." (John 5. 31.)

I beheld with ineffable awe our great Master's purpose in not questioning those he healed as to their disease, or its symptoms, and his marvelous skill in demanding neither obedience to hygienic laws nor prescribing drugs to support the divine power which heals. Adoringly I discerned the principle of his holy heroism and Christian example on the cross, when he refused to drink the "vinegar and gall," a preparation of poppy, or aconite, to allay the tortures of crucifixion.

Our great Way-shower, steadfast to the end in his obedience to God's laws, demonstrated for all time and peoples the supremacy of good over evil, and the superiority of Spirit over matter.

The miracles recorded in the Bible, which had before seemed to me supernatural, grew divinely natural and apprehensible, though uninspired interpreters ignorantly pronounce Christ's healing miraculous, instead of seeing therein the operation of the divine law.

Jesus of Nazareth was a natural and divine scientist. He was so before the material world saw him. He who antedated Abraham and gave the world a new date in the Christian era was a Christian Scientist who needed no discovery of the Science of Being in order to rebuke the evidence. To one "born of the flesh," however, Divine Science must be a discovery. Woman must give it birth. It must be begotten of spirituality, since none but the pure in heart can see God, the Principle of all things pure; and none but the "poor in spirit" could first state this principle, could know yet more of the nothingness of matter and the allness of Spirit, could utilize truth and absolutely reduce the demonstration of Being, in Science, to the apprehension of the age.

I wrote also, at this period, comments on the Scriptures, setting forth their spiritual interpretation, the science of the Bible, and so laid the foundation of my work called SCIENCE AND HEALTH, published in 1875.

2. Millenarianism Becomes Sectarian[1]

✦ *Ellen G. White*

The expectation of the second coming of Christ, accompanied by the Millennium — that is, a thousand-year reign of righteousness and peace — was once widely shared among the evangelical

---

[1] Ellen G. White, *The Great Controversy Between Christ and Satan* (Mountain View, Calif.: n.p., 1888), pp. 624–25, 657, 659, 662–66, 668.

*churches. When William Miller predicted that the appointed
time was close at hand, and indeed would come in 1844, there
was response from people of many denominations. But when the
predicted time came and went, there was a reaction, and millennial beliefs rapidly faded, except as they were still cherished by
small groups that made them their central doctrinal concern.
Among such groups, premillennialism was the usual version of
the doctrine — that is to say, the second coming is expected
before, not after, the Millennium itself. Christ will come amid
signs and portents; there will be a great conflict between Satan
and the hosts of Heaven, and Satan will be bound for a thousand
years; and then the Day of Judgment will arrive. Mrs. Ellen G.
White (1827–1915) was for many years the leading figure among
Seventh-Day Adventists, the most important of the religious
bodies directly descended from the Millerite agitation of the
1830's and 1840's.* ■

The Time of Trouble Is at Hand

Fearful sights of a supernatural character will soon be revealed in
the heavens, in token of the power of miracle-working demons. The
spirits of devils will go forth to the kings of the earth and to the
whole world, to fasten them in deception, and urge them on to
unite with Satan in his last struggle against the government of
heaven. By these agencies, rulers and subjects will be alike deceived.
Persons will arise pretending to be Christ himself, and claiming the
title and worship which belong to the world's redeemer. They will
perform wonderful miracles of healing, and will profess to have
revelations from heaven contradicting the testimony of the Scriptures.

Only those who have been diligent students of the Scriptures, and
who have received the love of the truth, will be shielded from the
powerful delusion that takes the world captive. By the Bible testimony these will detect the deceiver in his disguise. To all, the testing
time will come. By the sifting of temptation, the genuine Christian
will be revealed.

Christ's Second Coming

At the coming of Christ the wicked are blotted from the face of
the whole earth, consumed with the spirit of his mouth, and destroyed by the brightness of his glory. Christ takes his people to the
city of God, and the earth is emptied of its inhabitants.

132   *The Enlarging Pluralism*

The whole earth appears like a desolate wilderness. The ruins of cities and villages destroyed by the earthquake, uprooted trees, ragged rocks thrown out by the sea or torn out of the earth itself, are scattered over its surface, while vast caverns mark the spot where the mountains have been rent from their foundations.

Here is to be the home of Satan with his evil angels for a thousand years. Limited to the earth, he will not have access to other worlds to tempt and annoy those who have never fallen. It is in this sense that he is bound: there are none remaining upon whom he can exercise his power. He is wholly cut off from the work of deception and ruin which for so many centuries has been his sole delight.

The Last Mighty Struggle

At the close of the thousand years Christ again returns to the earth. He is accompanied by the host of the redeemed and attended by a retinue of angels. As he descends in terrific majesty, he bids the wicked dead arise to receive their doom. They come forth, a mighty host, numberless as the sands of the sea. What a contrast to those who were raised at the first resurrection! The righteous were clothed with immortal youth and beauty. The wicked bear the traces of disease and death.

Now Satan prepares for a last mighty struggle for the supremacy. While deprived of his power and cut off from his work of deception, the prince of evil was miserable and dejected; but as the wicked dead are raised and he sees the vast multitudes upon his side, his hopes revive, and he determines not to yield the great controversy. He will marshal all the armies of the lost under his banner, and through them endeavor to execute his plans.

At last the order to advance is given and the countless host moves on — an army such as was never summoned by earthly conquerors, such as the combined forces of all ages since war began on earth could never equal. Satan, the mightiest of warriors, leads the van, and his angels unite their forces for this final struggle. Kings and warriors are in his train, and the multitudes follow in vast companies, each under its appointed leader. With military precision, the serried ranks advance over the earth's broken and uneven surface to the city of God. By command of Jesus the gates of the New Jerusalem are closed and the armies of Satan surround the city and make ready for the onset.

Christ, Enthroned, Judges the Wicked

Now Christ again appears to the view of his enemies. Far above the city, upon a foundation of burnished gold, is a throne, high and lifted up. Upon this throne sits the son of God, and around him are the subjects of his kingdom. The power and majesty of Christ no language can describe, no pen portray. The glory of the Eternal Father is enshrouding his son. The brightness of his presence fills the city of God and flows out beyond the gates, flooding the whole earth with its radiance.

In the presence of the assembled inhabitants of earth and heaven the final coronation of the son of God takes place. And now, invested with supreme majesty and power, the King of kings pronounces sentence upon the rebels against his government and executes justice upon those who have transgressed his law and oppressed his people. Says the prophet of God: "I saw a great white throne, and him that sat on it, from whose face the earth and the heaven fled away; and there was found no place for them. And I saw the dead, small and great, stand before God; and the books were opened; and another book was opened, which is the book of life; and the dead were judged out of those things which were written in the books, according to their works."

The whole wicked world stands arraigned at the bar of God on the charge of high treason against the government of heaven. They have none to plead their cause; they are without excuse; and the sentence of eternal death is pronounced against them.

3. A Minority Demands Recognition[1]
✤ *William Cardinal O'Connell*

A small minority group is likely to accept it as a fact of life that it must accommodate itself in many ways to the patterns established by the majority. A growing minority is likely sooner or later to reach the point where it will insist that such one-way

[1] William Cardinal O'Connell, *Recollections of Seventy Years* (Boston: Houghton Mifflin, 1934), pp. 42–44.

accommodation violates its own integrity. Earlier selections have shown this shift in point of view on the part of members of the Roman Catholic Church. The selection that follows, describing Lowell, Massachusetts, in the 1870's shows this heightened self-consciousness and the interplay between its religious and its ethnic-group components. ■

One of the things, curiously enough, which helped to demonstrate the growing strength of the Catholic population in the city was the parade of the Irish Catholic men on the great feast of their patron saint. Early in the morning of Saint Patrick's Day the people flocked to their churches and listened to the triumphal strains of "Hail! Glorious Apostle," which wrought them up to a pitch of holy enthusiasm. After the High Mass the great procession was formed and, headed by bands and the floating banners of America and Ireland, thousands of men paraded through the principal streets, while the rest of the population looked on with mingled sentiments, the uppermost of which was surprise at the number and appearance of those men and boys, their faces aglow as they marched with sturdy stride over the long route. Here and there one caught a smile of derision on the faces of some of the onlookers. No doubt, to many the sight was not a welcome one. They endeavored to minimize its real importance by ridicule, but the marchers, young and old, with heads erect and eyes looking straight ahead as if into the future, felt that already the time had at last arrived when their existence, their power, and their numbers must be reckoned with. The bands played all along the route the wonderful marching tunes of the old Irish melodies, the most spirited of which was "Garry Owen," and even Sousa has never produced a better marching tune. Evening came and the celebration was continued at great public banquets, where in vivid oratory natural to the Irish were recalled all the glories, the triumphs, and the sufferings of the Irish race. The day of celebration ended with the prophecy of a glorious sunburst of long-awaited freedom for Ireland.

To the chagrin of the mill owners and managers, the workers made the seventeenth of March a great holiday, and to their wonder and one might say their anxiety as well, the machinery had to be stopped and the mill gates closed. When one remembers that this was not done in those times even on Christmas Day unless it happened to be

Sunday, the full significance of this closing of the mills on the feast day of a nation and the festival of a saint with which the mill-owners had, to say the least, extremely little sympathy, the full significance of the event, I say, will be quickly realized. The Irish Catholics of Lowell, by dint of vigorous, passive resistance, were beginning to win their rightful place and to force a reluctant recognition from those who hitherto had utterly ignored them and their human rights as citizens and workers.

Ethnic Variety in the Catholic Church

What we have said of the demonstration of Irish Catholics on the seventeenth of March was soon applicable to the French-Canadian Catholics, whose numbers, though still small comparatively, were continually on the increase. The Puritan had two grievances against the Irish Catholic, his race and his faith, both of which were traditionally the object of hatred and suspicion. The French Canadians, like the Irish before them, had to travel a hard road, but it was fairly well leveled and prepared for them by the early Irish immigrants. The antipathy toward the French was mostly because they were Catholics and, therefore, was only half of what was extended toward the Irish Catholics. Soon the French Canadians began to feel the need of a public demonstration of their numbers, and this had an outlet in the solemn celebration in their churches and their really beautiful parades on the feast of their patron saint, Saint Jean Baptiste. Somehow the Puritans looked with kindly eye upon these processions in honor of the precursor of our Lord, which was far different from the derisive enmity they showed the Apostle of Erin, whose very name was turned into ridicule.

Later came the Italians in far fewer numbers, and then the Portuguese and then the Poles, all Catholics. Each one of these groups observed, with outward demonstrations and parades, the festivals of its particular patron saint, and one began to see with wonderment the growing number of Catholic churches in various quarters of the city, filled to overflowing three or four times a Sunday with devout worshipers. As early as five in the morning one saw them by the thousands walking from their humble homes to their various parish churches, while in the meantime the Protestant churches were with great difficulty striving to hold a remnant of their once numerous congregations. The fair-minded non-Catholics, men and women, by constant contact and friendly relations with their neighbors, were beginning to realize that all the bitter controversial preaching from their pulpits was purposely concocted and propagated to stimulate the Protestants against showing any friendliness or even charity toward the newcomers. The honest and fair-minded people among them began to resent all this clap-trap as unworthy of a Christian minister and calculated only to disturb the peace of the city; and many henceforth frequented only those churches where they could hear the gospel of Christ's love for all and where no note of bitterness or petty hatred was ever sounded.

4. The "Yankee" Catholic Church[1]

✤ John Ireland

The adjustment that a minority makes to the ways of the dominant majority is not simply a reluctant acquiescence in a situation it has no power to change. Inevitably there will be some acceptance of the attitudes and patterns of behavior of the larger society. The extent to which the Roman Catholic Church should accommodate itself in this way to American life was a matter of controversy within that church in the latter part of the nineteenth century. The Americanist position was well stated by John Ireland, Archbishop of St. Paul, Minnesota, in commenting on the career of Isaac T. Hecker, the founder of the order of Paulist Fathers. ■

It is as clear to me as noonday light that countries and peoples have each their peculiar needs and aspirations as they have their peculiar environments, and that if we would enter into souls and control them, we must deal with them according to their conditions. The ideal line of conduct for the priest in Assyria will be out of all measure in Mexico or Minnesota, and I doubt not that one doing fairly well in Minnesota would by similar methods set things sadly astray in Leinster or Bavaria. The Saviour prescribed timeliness in pastoral caring. The master of a house, he said, "bringeth forth out of his treasury new things and old," as there is demand for one kind

[1] John Ireland, "Introduction" to Walter Elliott, *The Life of Father Hecker*, 4th ed. (New York: Columbus Press, 1898), pp. ix, x.

or the other. The apostles of nations, from Paul before the Areopagus to Patrick upon the summit of Tara, followed no different principle.

The circumstances of Catholics have been peculiar in the United States, and we have unavoidably suffered on this account. Catholics in largest numbers were Europeans, and so were their priests, many of whom — by no means all — remained in heart and mind and mode of action as alien to America as if they had never been removed from the Shannon, the Loire, or the Rhine. No one need remind me that immigration has brought us inestimable blessings, or that without it the Church in America would be of small stature. The remembrance of a precious fact is not put aside if I recall an accidental evil attaching to it. Priests foreign in disposition and work were not fitted to make favorable impressions upon the non-Catholic American population, and the American-born children of Catholic immigrants were likely to escape their action. And, lest I be misunderstood, I assert all this is as true of priests coming from Ireland as from any other foreign country. Even priests of American ancestry, ministering to immigrants, not unfrequently fell into the lines of those around them, and did but little to make the Church in America throb with American life. Not so Isaac Thomas Hecker. Whether consciously or unconsciously I do not know, and it matters not, he looked on America as the fairest conquest for divine truth, and he girded himself with arms shaped and tempered to the American pattern. I think that it may be said that the American current, so plain for the last quarter of a century in the flow of Catholic affairs, is, largely at least, to be traced back to Father Hecker and his early coworkers. It used to be said of them in reproach that they were the "Yankee" Catholic Church. The reproach was their praise.

5. The Eastern Orthodox Church[1]

✢ *Theodore Saloutos*

An "orthodox church," in the most general sense, is one that stresses the importance of correct doctrine. But the term "Orthodox Church" may also refer specifically to the churches of eastern Europe, which adhere to the doctrinal standards laid

[1] Theodore Saloutos, *The Greeks in the United States* (Cambridge: Harvard University Press, 1964), pp. 118–119, 122–123.

down by the seven ecumenical councils of the ancient church. The separation between the Roman Church and the Eastern or Orthodox Churches, made final in A.D. 1054, permitted significant differences to develop between Western and Eastern Christianity. When Americans encountered the Russian Orthodox Church or the Greek Orthodox Church, therefore, it was like meeting a distant cousin who was almost a stranger in the family. ■

Composed of many autonomous churches, the Eastern Orthodox Church was a sprawling organization whose teachings were based on the dogmas and canons set forth by the seven ecumenical councils. These autonomous churches included the Church of Constantinople, known to the Greeks as the Great Church or the Ecumenical Patriarchate, the Church of Antioch, the Church of Serbia, the Church of Romania, the Church of Georgia, the Church of Russia, and the Church of Greece. The administration of this extensive network of national churches can be compared to that of a religious confederation.

But to the Greeks in the United States it was the Church of Constantinople and the Church of Greece that were of greatest concern, for it was to these two branches of Orthodoxy that they owed their spiritual allegiance. Their religious lives were affected by what occurred within these two ecclesiastical jurisdictions: they furnished the first priests, shaped church policy in the Old World that in turn reacted on the churches in the New, and designated the hierarchs for the United States. Conflicts within these bodies and an inability to understand the problems of the immigrants compounded the difficulties of the local parishes.

There is significance in the fact that the Eastern Orthodox faith was introduced into the New World by the Russians. And it is relevant that the Eastern Orthodox Church, considered "the Mother of Christion churches," entered the United States from the western instead of the eastern end of the continent. Russian merchants and sailors who emigrated into Alaska from Siberia during the latter part of the eighteenth century planted its seeds in North American soil. After Alaska was purchased by the United States, the Russian church extended its missionary activities southward into the San Francisco area.

PLURALISM IN AMERICAN RELIGION: Diversity of belief has gone hand in hand with religious freedom. Although religious liberty was accepted by many as a matter of principle, it became a fact where religious pluralism made conformity to an established church impossible. In Maryland, for example, Catholics and Protestants early learned to live together peaceably. John Carroll (right) reorganized the Catholic Church in Maryland after the Revolution and became the first Roman Catholic bishop in the United States.

Freedom of religion not only allowed existing religions to flourish, it also permitted the development of several distinctively American religions. One of the earliest of these was begun by Joseph Smith in 1830 and was called the Church of Jesus Christ of Latter-Day Saints, or the Mormons. Because they held the Book of Mormon to be equal with the Bible in inspiration, and because they practiced polygamy, the Mormons were regarded with suspicion and animosity. The growing hostility toward them culminated in the sacking of the Mormon city of Nauvoo, Illinois, the remains of which are pictured at left.

Another American-born religion is the Church of Christ, Scientist, founded in 1879 by Mary Baker Eddy (right). In 1862, Mrs. Eddy, crippled by an accident, came under the influence of Phineas Quimby, a physician known for his belief in mental healing. Further studies led Mrs. Eddy to the conviction that all human sickness stems from a lack of spiritual understanding. Mrs. Eddy's writings and the Bible are the bases upon which Christian Science is founded.

Jews had settled this country in the seventeenth century, but their presence as a major force in the religious life of the nation was felt especially in the 1880's and after, when Jews emigrated here in large numbers from eastern Europe. They brought with them customs which seemed removed from the mainstream of American life. Sequestered in the tenements of New York and other cities, the forms and disciplines of the old faith served to draw Jews together into tightly knit communities. The orthodox rabbi (right) ministered to their needs and acted as the custodian of a great religious tradition. His attire, though a curiosity to non-Jews, was one indication that the ancient Jewish ways could resist the process of assimilation.

Not all branches of Judaism insisted on as strict an adherence to the Torah and Rabbinical Law as did the Orthodox. Conservative Judaism permitted some changes in ritual to meet the demands of modern living. Reform Judaism went still further in attempting to reconcile historical Judaism with modern life. Rabbi Isaac M. Wise (right) was a leading exponent of Reform Judaism in America, publishing a Reform newspaper and organizing the Union of American Hebrew Congregations. He urged a closer union between the Jewish faith and American ideals, while not sacrificing the determination of his people to remain distinctively Jewish in an increasingly homogeneous American society.

With the growth of immigration the Russian church shifted its headquarters eastward in an effort to minister more effectively to the needs of the newcomers. These churches in America came under the surveillance of the Church of Russia, whose political head was the tsar.

Greek Orthodoxy and Hellenism

Whenever the Greeks were too few in number to support a church of their own, and at a time when rivalries between the national churches in the country were nonexistent, they accepted, though reluctantly, the spiritual guidance of the Slavic churches and clergymen. But as soon as a sufficient number of Greeks settled in a particular community, their patriotic sentiments and national pride got the better of them. Then the Greek church, ministered to by a Greek priest, inevitably made its appearance. Relying on the Russians under such conditions was humiliating, a national disgrace. It was expecting too much for a proud and confident people, reared in a nationalistic atmosphere and owing allegiance to a state church, to content themselves with the spiritual leadership of a rival national church. This became unbearable later, after the flames of Greek nationalism had risen to full height.

In the United States Hellenism and Greek Orthodoxy — the one intertwined with the other — served as the cord that kept the immigrant attached to the mother country, nourished his patriotic appetites, and helped him preserve the faith and language of his parents. The receptiveness of the immigrant to this spirit cannot be underestimated. Absence from his ancestral home, the fear that he might never see it again, the thought of losing his nationality and of dying in a strange land, caused him, at least for a time, to embrace his religion with a fervor that he never had in Greece. He attended church because it reminded him of home. Neither a coercive government nor ecclesiastical decrees could have compelled these pioneers to maintain and administer their church communities with the turbulent aggressiveness that characterized them.

6. Orthodox Judaism[1]

✤ Hutchins Hapgood

A small number of Sephardic Jews (Spanish and Portuguese) settled in New Amsterdam in 1654; a considerable migration of Jews from Germany began before the Civil War. But it was the heavy migration from eastern Europe from the 1880s on that made the lower East Side of New York City, in Hutchins Hapgood's words, "the largest Jewish city in the world." Hapgood, not himself a Jew, wrote a sympathetic and understanding account of the traditional religious practices of orthodox Jews, so unlike the dominant Protestant patterns of religious behavior in this country. ■

No part of New York has a more intense and varied life than the colony of Russian and Galician Jews who live on the east side and who form the largest Jewish city in the world. The old and the new come here into close contact and throw each other into high relief. The traditions and customs of the orthodox Jew are maintained almost in their purity, and opposed to these are forms and ideas of modern life of the most extreme kind.

The Older Generation of Immigrants

Nevertheless these influences leave the man pretty much as he was when he landed here. He remains the patriarchal Jew devoted to the law and to prayer. He never does anything that is not prescribed, and worships most of the time that he is not at work. He has only one point of view, that of the Talmud;[2] and his aesthetic as well as his religious criteria are determined by it. "This is a beautiful letter you have written me," wrote an old man to his son, "it smells of Isaiah." He makes of his house a synagogue, and prays three times a day.

---

[1] Hutchins Hapgood, *The Spirit of the Ghetto* (New York: Funk & Wagnalls, 1902), pp. 9, 13–15, 17, 18, 23–24, 32.

[2] [**Talmud:** The collection of ancient writings by Jewish rabbis, consisting of (1) the *Mishnah* (oral interpretations of the Scriptures as compiled about A.D. 200) and (2) the *Gemara* (commentaries on the Mishnah). The Talmud is the basis of religious authority for traditional Judaism.]

When he prays his head is covered, he wears the black and white praying-shawl, and the cubes of the phylactery[3] are attached to his forehead and left arm. To the cubes are fastened two straps of goat-skin, black and white; those on the forehead hang down, and those attached to the other cube are wound seven times about the left arm. Inside each cube is a white parchment on which is written the Hebrew word for God, which must never be spoken by a Jew. The strength of this prohibition is so great that even the Jews who have lost their faith are unwilling to pronounce the word.

Besides the home prayers there are daily visits to the synagogue, fasts and holidays to observe. When there is a death in the family he does not go to the synagogue, but prays at home. The ten men necessary for the funeral ceremony, who are partly supplied by the Bereavement Committee of the Lodge, sit seven days in their stocking feet on footstools and read Job all the time. On the Day of Atonement the old Jew stands much of the day in the synagogue, wrapped in a white gown, and seems to be one of a meeting of the dead. The Day of Rejoicing of the Law and the Day of Purim are the only two days in the year when an orthodox Jew may be intoxicated. It is virtuous on these days to drink too much, but the sobriety of the Jew is so great that he sometimes cheats his friends and himself by shamming drunkenness. On the first and second evenings of the Passover the father dresses in a big white robe, the family gather about him, and the youngest male child asks the father the reason why the day is celebrated; whereupon the old man relates the whole history, and they all talk it over and eat and drink wine, but in no vessel which has been used before during the year, for everything must be fresh and clean on this day. The night before the Passover the remaining leavened bread is gathered together, just enough for breakfast, for only unleavened bread can be eaten during the next eight days. . . .

In spite, therefore, of his American environment, the old Jew of the ghetto remains patriarchal, highly trained and educated in a narrow sectarian direction, but entirely ignorant of modern culture; medieval, in effect, submerged in old tradition and outworn forms.

---

[3] [**phylactery:** Either of two small leather boxes, each containing strips of parchment inscribed with quotations from the Hebrew Scriptures. One is strapped to the forehead and the other to the left arm by observant Jewish men during morning worship, except on Sabbath and holidays.]

The Generation Gap

Whether born in this country or in Russia, the son of orthodox parents passes his earliest years in a family atmosphere where the whole duty of man is to observe the religious law. . . .

But in America, even before he begins to go to our public schools, the little Jewish boy finds himself in contact with a new world which stands in violent contrast with the orthodox environment of his first few years. . . .

With his entrance into the public school the little fellow runs plump against a system of education and a set of influences which are at total variance with those traditional to his race and with his home life. The religious element is entirely lacking. The educational system of the public schools is heterogeneous and worldly. . . .

The orthodox Jewish influences, still at work upon him, are rapidly weakened. He grows to look upon the ceremonial life at home as rather ridiculous. His old parents, who speak no English, he regards as "greenhorns." English becomes his habitual tongue even at home, and Yiddish he begins to forget. . . .

If this boy were able entirely to forget his origin, to cast off the ethical and religious influences which are his birthright, there would be no serious struggle in his soul, and he would not represent a peculiar element in our society. He would be like any other practical, ambitious, rather worldly American boy. The struggle is strong because the boy's nature, at once religious and susceptible, is strongly appealed to by both the old and new.

X. New Intellectual Challenges

The traditional view of the Bible as an infallible and unique revelation of God's will was seriously challenged in several ways. Darwin's theory of the origin of species could not be reconciled with the story of Creation in the book of Genesis; and Darwinism seemed to suggest that biological evolution had resulted, not from divine intelligence, but from the interplay of blind forces in nature. The Bible itself was more and more frequently considered to be a compilation of books by many authors, most of them anonymous, to be scrutinized in the same critical way as any other ancient writings. The assumption that Christianity is the one true religion was shaken by the realization that there are other great religious traditions, with their own sacred scriptures, ethical insights, and forms of worship. Among the various responses to these challenges to traditional Christian faith there may be distinguished (1) a conservative or "fundamentalist" rejection of them, (2) a radical or "humanist" acceptance of them and consequent abandonment of crucial aspects of the Christian tradition, and (3) a mediating attempt ("modernism") to reshape Christian doctrine in such a way as to accommodate new knowledge without casting aside old truths. ■

1. Darwinian Evolution[1]

✤ Andrew D. White

Although Charles Darwin, the author of The Origin of Species *(1859), once said that he saw no reason why his theories should shock the religious sensibilities of anyone, the fact is that their impact on religious faith and doctrine was sharp and lasting. Some of the high points in the controversy that resulted were*

---

[1] Andrew D. White, A *History of the Warfare of Science with Theology in Christendom* (New York: D. Appleton & Co., 1896), Vol. I, pp. 70–72, 79–82, 86.

*mentioned by the president of Cornell in a book which is itself
an important historical document.*   ■

Darwin's *Origin of Species* had come into the theological world
like a plough into an anthill. Everywhere those thus rudely awakened
from their old comfort and repose had swarmed forth angry and confused. Reviews, sermons, books light and heavy, came flying at the
new thinker from all sides.

The keynote was struck at once in the *Quarterly Review* by
Wilberforce, Bishop of Oxford. He declared that Darwin was guilty
of "a tendency to limit God's glory in creation," that "the principle of
natural selection is absolutely incompatible with the word of God,"
that it "contradicts the revealed relations of creation to its Creator,"
that it is "inconsistent with the fulness of his glory," that it is "a
dishonouring view of nature," and that there is "a simpler explanation of the presence of these strange forms among the works of God"
— that explanation being "the fall of Adam." Nor did the bishop's
efforts end here. At the meeting of the British Association for the
Advancement of Science he again disported himself in the tide of
popular applause. Referring to the ideas of Darwin, who was absent
on account of illness, he congratulated himself in a public speech
that he was not descended from a monkey. The reply came from
Huxley, who said in substance: "If I had to choose, I would prefer
to be a descendant of a humble monkey rather than of a man who
employs his knowledge and eloquence in misrepresenting those who
are wearing out their lives in the search for truth."

This shot reverberated through England, and indeed through other
countries.

American Reactions

Echoes came from America. One review, the organ of the most
widespread of American religious sects, declared that Darwin was
"attempting to befog and to pettifog the whole question," another
denounced Darwin's views as "infidelity," another, representing the
American branch of the Anglican Church, poured contempt over
Darwin as "sophistical and illogical," and then plunged into an exceedingly dangerous line of argument in the following words: "If this
hypothesis be true, then is the Bible an unbearable fiction; . . . then

have Christians for nearly two thousand years been duped by a monstrous lie. . . . Darwin requires us to disbelieve the authoritative word of the Creator." . . .

But a far more determined opponent was the Rev. Dr. Hodge of Princeton; his anger toward the evolution doctrine was bitter. He denounced it as thoroughly "atheistic." He insisted that Christians "have a right to protest against the arraying of probabilities against the clear evidence of the Scriptures." He even censured so orthodox a writer as the Duke of Argyll, and declared that the Darwinian theory of natural selection is "utterly inconsistent with the Scriptures," and that "an absent God, who does nothing, is to us no God," that "to ignore design as manifested in God's creation is to dethrone God," that "a denial of design in nature is virtually a denial of God," and that "no teleologist[2] can be a Darwinian." Even more uncompromising was another of the leading authorities at the same university — the Rev. Dr. Duffield. He declared war not only against Darwin but even against men like Asa Gray, Le Conte, and others, who had attempted to reconcile the new theory with the Bible. He insisted that "evolutionism and the Scriptural account of the origin of man are irreconcilable" — that the Darwinian theory is "in direct conflict with the teaching of the apostle, 'All scripture is given by inspiration of God.'" He pointed out, in his opposition to Darwin's *Descent of Man* and Lyell's *Antiquity of Man*, that in the Bible "the genealogical links which connect the Israelites in Egypt with Adam and Eve in Eden are explicitly given." These utterances of Prof. Duffield culminated in a declaration which deserves to be cited as showing that a Presbyterian minister can "deal damnation round the land" . . . in a fashion quite equal to that of popes and bishops. It is as follows: "If the development theory of the origin of man," wrote Dr. Duffield in the *Princeton Review*, "shall in a little while take its place — as doubtless it will — with other exploded scientific speculations, then they who accept it with its proper logical consequences will in the life to come have their portion with those who in this life 'know not God and obey not the gospel of his Son.'"

Fortunately, at about the time when Darwin's *Descent of Man* was published, there had come into Princeton University a *deus ex*

---

[2] [**teleologist**: one who believes that natural processes are not determined by mechanism, but by an overall design or purpose in the universe.]

machina[3] in the person of Dr. James McCosh. Called to the presidency, he at once took his stand against teachings so dangerous to Christianity as those of Drs. Hodge, Duffield, and their associates. In one of his personal confidences he has let us into the secret of this matter. With that hard Scotch sense which Thackeray had applauded in his well-known verses, he saw that the most dangerous thing which could be done to Christianity at Princeton was to reiterate in the university pulpit, week after week, solemn declarations that if evolution by natural selection, or indeed evolution at all, be true, the Scriptures are false. He tells us that he saw that this was the certain way to make the students unbelievers; he therefore not only checked this dangerous preaching but preached an opposite doctrine. With him began the inevitable compromise, and, in spite of mutterings against him as a Darwinian, he carried the day.

Theology Rethought in the Light of Evolutionary Biology

Other divines of strong sense in other parts of the country began to take similar ground — namely, that men could be Christians and at the same time Darwinians. . . .

In view of the proofs accumulating in favor of the new evolutionary hypothesis, the change in the tone of controlling theologians was now rapid. From all sides came evidences of desire to compromise with the theory.

Whatever additional factors may be added to natural selection — and Darwin himself fully admitted that there might be others — the theory of an evolution process in the formation of the universe and of animated nature is established, and the old theory of direct creation is gone forever. In place of it science has given us conceptions far more noble, and opened the way to an argument for design infinitely more beautiful than any ever developed by theology.

[3] [**deus ex machina**: "god from a machine" (Latin) — an unexpected solution to a difficult problem]

2. Biblical Criticism[1]

♣ Peter H. Steenstra

*The critical study of the Bible, which had concerned scholars
for more than a century, especially in Germany, began to be a
matter of widespread discussion in the churches in the latter part
of the nineteenth century. Churchmen who had always taken it
for granted that Moses wrote the first five books and that David
wrote the Psalms found such traditional views challenged. But if
the Bible is to be regarded as a book to be analyzed like other
books written by men, parts of it rejected as spurious, and parts
of it dismissed as scientifically inaccurate, in what sense can it be
regarded as a revelation from God? A professor in the Episcopal
Theological School in Cambridge, Massachusetts, recalls at the
close of his teaching career the transformation that had come
about in the way men regarded the Bible.* ■

And yet my forty years here, looked at from the inside, have been
eventful in one respect at least. During that forty years there has been
a great transition in theological thought — in theological thought
with respect to that which forms the basis, has furnished and still must
furnish the basis of theological thinking, the Bible. This was indeed a
great transition — a transition the greatness of which I believe few of
us yet understand — the bearing of which upon the practical life and
teaching of the Church, I believe, few of us yet comprehend. And
the mediation of that transition within the limits of this school it was
both my task and my privilege to conduct. It was *an event* of which
I think few theological teachers have experience: an event to me, an
event to my students, an event which in the very nature of the case
can hardly be repeated once in a century.

When I came here I was under the still strong influence of the old
theory about the Bible. What was that theory? To put it in one
word, it was the idea of a book revelation. God had revealed himself

[1] Peter H. Steenstra, Remarks at the Fortieth Anniversary Alumni Banquet,
Episcopal Theological School, June 4, 1907. Quoted in George L. Blackman,
Faith and Freedom, pp. 295–297. Copyright © 1967 by The Seabury Press,
Incorporated. Reprinted by permission of The Seabury Press and the Episcopal
Theological School, Cambridge, Massachusetts.

to us, and that revelation was in the book, that revelation was the book, and that book had been written by infallibly inspired men.

I had difficulties with these two conceptions from the time I was twenty years old, and I had them when I came here. For thirty years I was turning over all that I could lay hands on of what had been written — in Germany, of course — on the origin of the Pentateuch. For there the battle began. Its results of course took in the whole Old Testament. Fought out there, it was fought out for the Bible as a whole.

For long years I felt that to talk of infallible inspiration was to talk of what, psychologically speaking, was an impossibility. Even almighty power cannot inspire a man infallibly unless he converts the man into a mere typewriting machine. Given a prophet, given a man, a thinking man, a feeling man, a man who looks back, a man who looks forward, a man who looks sideways — *that* man, inspired as he may be, can never be inspired infallibly.

Wellhausen's Critical Work

These questions were discussed, and the analysis of the Pentateuch was carried on year after year, and resulted in book after book, and theory after theory. One thing about it: all the theories agreed that Moses did not write the Pentateuch, that the Psalms were not written by David (at least, most of them were not), and that in the historical part of the Old Testament — even in the oldest portions of it, there were a great many inaccuracies, inaccuracies not merely of science, but in history. And it was not until Wellhausen[2] published his epoch-making book that we really got light on the subject.

You see, all this work had been something like the making of a card picture by a child, or a map cut up into forty pieces — which pieces the child tries to arrange in such a way as to give the complete, true, and accurate form of the map.

It was, however, several decades before Wellhausen wrote that the solution was suggested in the University of Strassburg by Reuss. The suggestion heard there by one of his pupils, Graf, was by him worked

---

[2] [**Wellhausen:** Julius Wellhausen (1844–1918), German Biblical scholar, whose persuasive statement of the conclusions to which the work of many scholars had contributed made him a leading exponent of the new views of the Bible, and therefore sharply criticized by the conservatives.]

out afterwards, presented in various forms by several other men, and finally demonstrated to be true by its results by Wellhausen, who undertook to compare the results of the literary analysis with the historical notices both in the historical and the prophetical books of the Old Testament. That threw light over the whole. That was really the liberating book, even though Wellhausen did not originate the theory. Reuss had seen the whole thing — had in fact instigated the successful process. But no one had worked it out with such convincing power and force as Wellhausen. The moment I read his book, I had the answer and the solution of all my doubts and difficulties; and for the last twenty years I have been trying to impart what I had learned to the successive classes of this school.

And now, I want to say one more word in closing, and that is this: Do not imagine for a moment that this transition from one view of the Bible to another view necessitates a doubt or uncertainty as to Christianity. A good many people, of course, are afraid it does; but it isn't so. The more I study the history of the way in and through which God revealed himself to the Hebrew people, and through them to the world; the more I study the history which began in Ur of the Chaldees (a city, not of Babylonia, but — as I am persuaded — of North Mesopotamia), and led up and up and up until it culminated in the Christ; the more I feel that that history is its own self-sufficient guarantee.

3. The World's Parliament of Religions[1]

✤ *Charles W. Wendte*

The nineteenth century brought to Americans an increased knowledge of other parts of the world and a fresh awareness of religious traditions other than Christianity. Instead of the lands beyond the seas being populated, vaguely, by "heathen" who needed to be converted, they were found to have rich religious cultures and ancient sacred scriptures of their own. For many, the result was to bring in question the exclusive claim of Christianity to be the one divinely appointed true religion. No event

[1] John Henry Barrows, *The World's Parliament of Religions* (Chicago: Parliament Publishing Co., 1893). Vol. I, pp. 62, 64.

more strikingly expressed the new mood than the World's Parliament of Religions in Chicago (1893). The opening session is here described. ■

Long before the appointed hour the building swarmed with delegates and visitors, and the Hall of Columbus was crowded with four thousand eager listeners from all parts of the country and foreign lands. At 10 o'clock there marched down the aisle arm in arm, the representatives of a dozen world faiths, beneath the waving flags of many nations, and amid the enthusiastic cheering of the vast audience. The platform at this juncture presented a most picturesque and impressive spectacle. In the center, clad in scarlet robes and seated in a high chair of state, was Cardinal Gibbons, the highest prelate of his church in the United States, who, as was fitting in this Columbian year, was to open the meeting with prayer.

On either side of him were grouped the Oriental delegates, whose many-colored raiments vied with his own in brilliancy. Conspicuous among these followers of Brahma and Buddha and Mohammed was the eloquent monk Vivekananda of Bombay, clad in gorgeous red apparel, his bronzed face surmounted with a huge turban of yellow. Beside him, attired in orange and white, sat B. B. Nagarkar of the Brahmo-Somaj, or association of Hindu Theists, and Dharmapala, the learned Buddhist scholar from Ceylon, who brought the greetings of four hundred and seventy-five millions of Buddhists, and whose slight, lithe person was swathed in pure white, while his black hair fell in curls upon his shoulders.

There were present, also, Mohammedan and Parsee and Jain ecclesiastics, each a picturesque study in color and movement, and all eager to explain and defend their forms of faith.

The most gorgeous group was composed of the Chinese and Japanese delegates, great dignitaries in their own country, arrayed in costly silk vestments of all the colors of the rainbow, and officially representing the Buddhist, Taoist, Confucian and Shinto forms of worship.

In dark, almost ascetic garb, there sat among his fellow Orientals, Protab Chunder Mozoomdar. Mr. Mozoomdar, the leader of the Brahmo-Somaj or Hindoo Theists in India, visited this country some years since, and delighted large audiences with his eloquence and perfect command of the English tongue.

Another striking figure was the Greek Archbishop of Zante, his venerable beard sweeping his chest, his head crowned with a strange looking hat, leaning on a quaintly carved staff, and displaying a large silver cross suspended from his girdle.

A ruddy-cheeked, long-locked Greek monk from Asia Minor, who sat by his side, boasted that he had never yet worn a head-covering or spent a penny of his own for food or shelter.

The ebon-hued but bright faces of Bishop Arnett, of the African Methodist Church, and of a young African prince, were relieved by the handsome costumes of the ladies of the company, while forming a somber background to all was the dark raiment of the Protestant delegates and invited guests.

4. Conservatism, or Fundamentalism[1]

✦ *J. Gresham Machen*

> *How should one respond to the newer ways of looking at the origins of mankind, the nature of the Bible, and the spiritual riches of non-Christian religions? There were those who said that no real reconciliation is possible between Christian truth and these new notions, and resolved to take a stand on certain traditional "fundamentals" of the Christian faith. One of the ablest spokesmen for this conservatism was J. Gresham Machen, a Presbyterian, who taught for many years at Princeton Theological Seminary. In 1929, he resigned his professorship there to help organize Westminister Theological Seminary as an unambiguously conservative school.* ■

In my little book, *Christianity and Liberalism*, 1923, I tried to show that the issue in the Church of the present day is not between two varieties of the same religion, but, at bottom, between two essentially different types of thought and life. There is much interlocking of the branches, but the two tendencies, modernism and supernaturalism, or (otherwise designated) nondoctrinal religion and historic Christianity, spring from different roots.

[1] Vergilius Ferm, ed., *Contemporary American Theology*, Vol. I (New York: Round Table Press, 1932), pp. 266–273.

Conservatism Loses Control of Princeton Seminary

The period of twenty-seven years during which, with two short intervals, I was connected first as student and then as teacher with Princeton Theological Seminary, witnessed the conflict between the old Princeton and the newer forces now dominant in the Presbyterian Church; and finally it witnessed the triumph of the latter in the reorganization of the seminary in 1929. . . .

The old Princeton Seminary first resisted, then succumbed to, the drift of the times. It did not succumb of its own free will; for the majority of its governing board as well as the majority of its faculty desired to maintain the old policy; but that board was removed by the General Assembly of the Presbyterian Church in 1929 and another board was placed in control. Thus the future conformity of Princeton Seminary to the general drift of the times was insured. . . .

When the reorganization of Princeton Seminary took place, some men felt that so fine a scholarly tradition as that of the old Princeton ought not to be allowed to perish from the earth. Obviously it could not successfully be continued at Princeton, under the new and unsympathetic board, but elsewhere it might be carried on.

It is being carried on at the new Westminster Theological Seminary in Philadelphia, which was founded in 1929, largely through the initiative of self-sacrificing laymen, "to carry on and perpetuate the policies and traditions of Princeton Theological Seminary, as it existed prior to the reorganization thereof in 1929, in respect to scholarship and militant defense of the Reformed Faith."

Christianity Susceptible of Rational Defence

There are certain root convictions which I hold in common with Westminster Seminary and with the journal *Christianity Today* — in common with these representatives of the ancient yet living tradition of the old Princeton. I hold (1) that the Christian religion, as it is set forth on the basis of Holy Scripture in the Standards of the Reformed Faith, is true, and (2) that the Christian religion as so set forth requires and is capable of scholarly defense.

The former of these two convictions makes me dislike the term "fundamentalism." If, indeed, I am asked whether I am a fundamentalist or a modernist, I do not say, "Neither." I do not quibble. In that disjunction, as the inquirer means it, I have very definitely taken sides. But I do not apply the term "fundamentalist" to myself. I stand, indeed, in the very warmest Christian fellowship with those who do designate themselves by that term. But, for my part, I cannot see why the Christian religion, which has had a rather long and honorable history, should suddenly become an "-ism" and be called by a strange new name.

The second of the two convictions just formulated — that the Christian religion requires and is capable of scholarly defense — does not mean that a man ever was made a Christian merely by argument. There must also be the mysterious work of the Spirit of God in the new birth. But because argument is insufficient it does not follow that it is unnecessary. From the very beginning, true Christianity has always been presented as a thoroughly reasonable thing. . . . Real Christianity is no mere form of mysticism, but is founded squarely upon a body of truth. . . .

I take a grave view of the present state of the Church. I think that those who cry, " 'Peace, peace,' when there is no peace," constitute the greatest menace to the people of God. . . . Those who form the consistently Christian remnant in the Presbyterian Church and in other churches, instead of taking refuge in a cowardly anti-intellectualism, instead of decrying controversy, ought to be on their knees asking God to bring the visible Church back from her wanderings to her true Lord.

5. Modernism[1]

✦ Harry Emerson Fosdick

The Reverend Harry Emerson Fosdick found himself in the midst of controversy in 1922 when he preached a sermon entitled: "Shall the Fundamentalists Win?" Fosdick, though a Baptist, was then minister of a Presbyterian church in New York City. Although his own congregation stood by him, he finally resigned and became minister of the interdenominational Riverside Church in New York. ■

[1] Abridged from pp. 144–145, 146, 152, 157, 162, 163 in *The Living of These Days* by Harry Emerson Fosdick. Copyright © 1956 by Harper & Row, Publishers, Inc. Reprinted by permission of the publishers.

The conflict between liberal and reactionary Christianity had long been moving toward a climax. . . .

When the storm did break, chance placed me near the center, and I tell the story of the controversy, as I experienced it, not because my share in it was more important than many others', but because I did have an interesting opportunity to see it from the inside.

The Fundamentalist Controversy

My sermon, "Shall the Fundamentalists Win?" was a plea for tolerance, for a church inclusive enough to take in both liberals and conservatives without either trying to drive the other out. I stated the honest differences of conviction dividing these two groups on such matters as the virgin birth of Jesus, the inerrancy of the Scriptures and the second coming of Christ, and then made my plea that the desirable solution was not a split that would tear the evangelical churches asunder, but a spirit of conciliation that would work out the problem within an inclusive fellowship.

If ever a sermon failed to achieve its object, mine did. It was a plea for good will, but what came of it was an explosion of ill will, for over two years making headline news of a controversy that went the limit of truculence. The trouble was, of course, that in stating the liberal and fundamentalist positions, I had stood in a Presbyterian pulpit and said frankly what the modernist position on some points was — the virgin birth no longer accepted as historic fact, the literal inerrancy of the Scriptures incredible, the second coming of Christ from the skies an outmoded phrasing of hope.

Three Disputing Groups

Meanwhile, as the months passed the controversial uproar grew ever louder and more obstreperous across the country. . . . My own situation became correspondingly warm, with three groups throwing fagots on the flame.

First, the fundamentalists themselves grew increasingly vehement. In pulpits, magazines, pamphlets and mass meetings they assailed the liberals and called on them to leave the evangelical churches. Their slogan was concisely stated in a mass meeting of Presbyterian fundamentalists in New York: "We have a right to demand that those who serve as pastors of our churches shall 'hew to the line' in matters of faith.". . .

The second party in the conflict was made up of my friends. They did not all agree with me doctrinally, but they were in general on the liberal side, and in particular were deeply concerned about maintaining personal freedom in the church. The outcome that would follow a fundamentalist victory was clear. As one typical Presbyterian reactionary put it: "How can men who are honest stay in the Presbyterian Church when they no longer believe in her doctrines? There is only one honest way for these brethren to act. Let them get out!" This meant, however, that the church's doctrines were finally to be frozen in terms which the fundamentalists chose and that both all liberty of interpretation and all possibility of progress were to be denied. . . .

It was not alone the fundamentalists and liberals, however, who heated the fires of controversy; a third group, small in number but vociferous in expression, added to its vehemence. This group was made up of left-wing religious radicals. Many of them had been ministers or members of evangelical churches, and finding the constraints intolerable had left them. They took the same position the fundamentalists did on one point: that the liberals should leave the evangelical denominations. Common honesty, they thought, demanded that the liberals get out. No criticism of my attitude from the fundamentalists was more harsh than some that came from this left-wing group. They insisted that my only decent course was to do as they had done — shake the dust of the evangelical denominations from my feet.

The difference in point of view between the evangelical liberals and this left-wing group was important. The radicals, motivated by disgust with the evangelical churches, wanted them left to their own hidebound, obscurantist devices. We, on the other hand, were determined not to surrender to the fundamentalists the control of the great historic denominations. We saw in them priceless values; we treasured the Christian heritage of which, with all their faults, they were the most influential conservers; we felt ourselves one with them in the abiding, substantial truths they stood for, despite our disagreement with their outgrown theological formulas. For all the liberals to desert them, leaving their long-accumulated prestige, their powerful influence and their multitudes of devoted Christian people in the hands of fundamentalist leadership, seemed to us an unthinkable surrender and an intolerable tragedy to the Christian cause.

XI. Some Recent Tendencies

No one can ever be certain which of the currents and cross-currents of his own day will ultimately prove to have been decisive. No selection of material can therefore be made with any finality. Yet it looks as though the ecumenical movement, which seeks to draw together the divided denominations, is an authentic expression of our times; and it is clear that the story of these days can hardly be told without full attention to the growing self-consciousness and influence of the black community. ■

1. Church Union Among Protestants[1]

✤ Consultation on Church Union

Throughout the nineteenth century, the occasions when denominations split over doctrinal, political, or social issues were many, while the occasions when divided denominations came together were few. A different mood has prevailed in our own day. There have been numerous mergers involving two or three denominations, usually ones with similar backgrounds. The most ambitious attempt at church union, which would bring together Protestant denominations of somewhat different backgrounds, has been under discussion since the early 1960's. Known as the Consultation on Church Union (COCU), it has involved active negotiation, the final outcome of which is still in the future. The intent of the sponsors was stated in 1966 in the excerpt that follows. ■

We are convinced that the characteristics of the Church which are God's gifts to it can be fully seen only as the Church becomes

---

[1] *Digest of the Proceedings of the Fifth Meeting of the Consultation on Church Union. Held at Dallas, Texas, May 2–5, 1966.* (n.p., n.d.) pp. 38–39.

visibly one. The Communion which is his gift to broken humanity, the holiness which marks his actions in us and among us, the catholicity which names what is always and everywhere accepted by Christians, the apostolicity which assures the identity of the Church across the centuries and links us to Christ's mission from the beginning — all these we hold essential and dear; but we know that they can be fully manifested only as the Church itself is plainly united. Above all, the gracious gifts of the Holy Spirit which empower the heroic obedience and witness of Christians can be fully honored only in and by a church which is whole and one. In forming this united and uniting church, we express our thankfulness for these gifts, and seek so to order our common life that they may be manifested more clearly.

We recognize the presence and reality of the one Church within the life of each of the constituting churches. The act of unification we propose is in part a sign of this mutual recognition based on the deeper recognition of the reality of God's gifts to each.

We resolve to attempt, under God, a more inclusive expression of the oneness of the Church of Christ than any of the participating churches can suppose itself alone to be. This inclusiveness means several things. It means an increase in corporate strength not alone in numbers but also in the vitality of common witness. It means a new richness of tradition in which none will lose and all will gain through the discovery of diverse ways of praising God, learning about him, following him and making him known. It means more extensive and intimate relationships with other Christian bodies and with the wide sweep of human society — relationships which simply are not open to churches in isolation. It means enhanced ability to manifest the fullness of the Church's life and obedience to the divine mission. And in all this, our desire for greater inclusiveness is primarily based on the knowledge that God's will is resisted and denied by separations which make it impossible for us to worship and work as one communion in Christ. The separations themselves, when they came about, undoubtedly expressed true obedience to conscience. It is this same obedience which now calls us to unity more inclusive and more relevant to God's evident purposes in our time.

We resolve to attempt, under God, a truer expression of the fullness of the Church of Christ than any of the constituting churches can suppose itself to be. This includes a fidelity to God's revelation in the Scriptures greater than when churches merely appeal to the Bible's words to justify their separate ways and refuse to allow the same covenant to yoke them together in common tasks. It includes a more adequate and credible confession of faith than can be the case where separate traditions obscure the common inheritance. It includes a public worship and sacramental life which will manifest more clearly and surely the high priesthood of Christ, and the part of all believers in that priesthood, than is possible behind walls of separation which exclude some of those whom Christ has welcomed. It includes an ordering of the ministry which will recognize a greater diversity of the Spirit's gifts, and release those gifts for wider and more effective service, than is the case where separated ministries in separated churches are expected to give priority to the institutional interests of those churches. Thus we, humbly and penitently, seek to create the conditions for a fuller expression of the faith, the worship, the ministry, and the mission of the one Church of Christ.

2. Catholic Ecumenism[1]

✣ *Bishops' Commission for Ecumenical Affairs*

Protestant-Catholic relations have been profoundly affected of late by the Second Vatican Council, convened by Pope John XXIII. The Council revealed that the Roman Catholic Church was responding to situations and problems with which Protestants were also concerned, and the Pope's transparent love for all sorts and conditions of men made it easier for Protestants to forget old barriers of exclusiveness. In June, 1965, shortly after the Council approved its Decree on Ecumenism, the American bishops issued a set of guidelines for future relationships with Protestant churches, including common participation in occasions of worship. Where once such a document would have been restrictive in tone, and would have sought to minimize contacts, the new mood was affirmative, despite a reminder of the prescribed limits within which co-operation was regarded as appropriate. ∎

[1] "Interim Guidelines for Prayer in Common and *Communicatio in Sacris*," reprinted in Hiley Ward, *Documents of Dialogue* (Englewood Cliffs, N.J.: Prentice Hall, 1966), pp. 111–112.

In accordance with Section 8 of the Decree on Ecumenism the participation of Catholics with other Christians in services which are not part of the official liturgies of any communion, if these services are devoted to the cause of Christian unity, is highly desirable. Such services could fittingly be called "Ecumenical Services." Participation of Catholics in such services, whether they are held for the sake of promoting Christian unity in accordance with the Decree or, in the spirit of the Decree, for some other purpose, e.g., for peace, in time of public need, mourning, thanksgiving, etc., remains under the guidance of the local bishop.

The place chosen for the conduct of these ecumenical services should provide a worthy setting which is acceptable to all the participants and which, according to the prudent decision of the local bishop, is considered suitable. With the approval of the local bishop priests are to be encouraged to take an active part in the conduct of services, e.g. by reading Scripture lessons, preaching homilies, offering prayers and giving blessings.

The vesture to be worn at such services is also to be determined by the local bishop. In some circumstances ordinary civil attire may be the only appropriate form of dress for the participating priest. In other circumstances, since it is in accordance with Catholic usage even in the conduct of nonliturgical services, the use of the cassock and surplice may be considered. Another form of dress which is neither liturgical nor merely civil, namely, the use of the ferraiuola,[2] may be desirable on certain occasions. The value of some kind of "sacred" vesture is not to be underestimated in creating the right atmosphere for prayer in common. In reaching decisions concerning ecclesiastical vesture on these occasions it is highly recommended that there be consultation with the clergy of the other church bodies which are to participate in such services.

On occasion members of the Catholic laity may also be invited to take an active part in Ecumenical Services. They may, for example, be called upon to read the Scripture lessons.

Under the guidance of the local bishop, who may well wish to consult his ecumenical commission regarding the qualifications of the

[2] [**ferraiuola**: a mantle or cloak.]

laity invited to take these leading roles, such participation on the part of laymen has much to recommend it. The acceptance of such a policy could become one more manifestation of the Church's doctrine on the laity as found in the Constitution on the Church.

In preparing for and conducting these Ecumenical Services the principle of "reciprocity" should be kept in mind: to accept an invitation may often seem to entail an obligation to extend a similar invitation and to proffer an invitation may imply a readiness to receive one; one should not, therefore, accept an invitation if, according to Catholic norms, one cannot proffer a similar invitation.

All such joint services of prayer should be carefully prepared in accordance with the principle of "collaboration." The leaders of the participating groups should, after careful consideration, agree on the format of the services and on the choice of themes, Scripture reading and hymns. Prayers and hymns and homilies which may be unacceptable either to Catholics or to other Christians are to be avoided.

These ecumenical services, it is hoped, will complement the programs of prayer for unity which continue in our churches.

3. The "American Way of Life" as a Secular Faith[1]
✦ *Will Herberg*

The ecumenical movement understands there to be values held in common by all Christians, even though social forces have fragmented the Church as an institution. Ecumenism is the way by which some American churchmen have sought to strengthen the forces making for unity and coherence in a pluralistic society. But even a reunion of all branches of the Christian church would not include all Americans. And so a modern sociologist argues that the "three faiths" — Protestant, Catholic, Jewish — are in fact coming to be alternative modes of a secular American faith, the "American Way of Life." ■

[1] Will Herberg, "Religion and Culture in Present-Day America," in Thomas T. McAvoy, *Roman Catholicism and the American Way of Life* (Notre Dame: University of Notre Dame Press, 1960), pp. 7–8, 11–13.

oday, to be born an American is no longer taken to mean that one is necessarily a Protestant; Protestantism is no longer the obvious and "natural" religious identification of the American. Today, the evidence strongly indicates, America has become a three-religion country: the normal religious implication of being an American today is that one is either a Protestant, a Catholic, or a Jew. These three are felt to be, by and large, three different forms of being religious in the American way; they are the three "religions of democracy," the "three great faiths" of America. . . .

Just as Americans are coming more and more to think of being a Protestant, being a Catholic, and being a Jew as three alternative ways of being an American, so they are coming to regard Protestantism, Catholicism, and Judaism, the "three great faiths," as three alternative (though not necessarily equal) expressions of a great overarching commitment which they all share by virtue of being Americans. This commitment is, of course, democracy or the American Way of Life. It is the common allegiance which (to use Professor Williams' phrase) provides Americans with the "common set of ideas, rituals, and symbols" through which an "overarching sense of unity" is achieved amidst diversity and conflict.[2] It is, in a sense far more real than John Dewey ever dreamed of, the "common religion" of Americans.

Let me illustrate this point with two texts borrowed from President Eisenhower, who may, I think, be taken as a representative American really serious about religion. "Our government," Mr. Eisenhower declared shortly after his election in 1952, "makes no sense unless it is founded in a deeply-felt religious faith, *and I don't care what it is*."[3] It is the last phrase which I have emphasized — 'and I don't care what it is' — to which I want to call your attention. Of course, President Eisenhower did not mean that literally; he would have been much disturbed had any sizable proportion of Americans become Buddhists, or Shintoists, or Confucianists — but of course that never entered his mind. When he said "I don't care what it is," he ob-

---

[2] Robin M. Williams, Jr., *American Society: A Sociological Interpretation* (Knopf, 1951), p. 312.

[3] *New York Times*, December 23, 1952.

viously meant "I don't care which of the three it is — Protestantism, Catholicism, or Judaism." And why didn't he care which it was? Because, in his view, as in the view of all normal Americans, they "all say the same thing." And what is the "same thing" which they all say? The answer is given to us from the current vocabulary: "the moral and spiritual values of democracy." These, for the typical American, are in a real sense final and ultimate; the three conventional religions are approved of and validated primarily because they embody and express these "moral and spiritual values of democracy."

Let me drive this home with the second text from President Eisenhower. In 1948, four years before his election, just before he became president of Columbia, Mr. Eisenhower made another important pronouncement on religion. "I am the most intensely religious man I know," he declared. "Nobody goes through six years of war without faith. That does not mean that I adhere to any sect. (Incidentally, following the way of all flesh, he was soon to join a "sect," the Presbyterian.) A democracy cannot exist without a religious base. I believe in democracy."[4] Here we have the entire story in a single phrase: I believe in religion because I believe in democracy! . . .

What I am describing is essentially the "Americanization" of religion in America, and therefore also its thorough-going secularization.

[4] *New York Times*, May 4, 1948.

4. Aspects of Black Religion[1]

✤ Malcolm X

A disadvantaged group, alienated from the surrounding society, often seeks to create its own religious institutions. Sometimes these will take the form of small sects within the dominant religious culture; sometimes, as with the Black Muslims, there will be an attempt to reject that culture. Yet the carryover from the old to the new — in this case from Christianity to the religion of Islam — is likely to be great. The address from which this selection is taken has many accents of evangelical religion, including a version of the Millennium at the close. It should be noted

[1] Archie Epps, ed., *The Speeches of Malcolm X at Harvard* (New York: William Morrow, 1968), pp. 116, 130–31.

*that when Malcolm X delivered this address in 1961 he was a
prominent figure among the Black Muslims; but before his
assassination in 1965, he had broken with the Honorable Elijah
Muhammad, the Muslim leader, and moved away from the principle of complete separation of the races.* ■

To understand our views, the views of the Muslims, you must first
realize that we are a religious group, and you must also know something about our religion, the religion of Islam. The creator of the
universe, whom many of you call God or Jehovah, is known to the
Muslims by the name Allah. The Muslims believe there is but one
God, and that all the prophets came from this one God. . . . One who
practices divine obedience is called a Muslim. . . . There are over
seven hundred twenty-five million Muslims on this earth, predominantly in Africa and Asia, the nonwhite world.

Separation of the Races

Mr. Elijah Muhammad is our divine leader and teacher here in
America. . . . We who follow Mr. Muhammad know that he has been
divinely taught and sent to us by God himself. We believe that the
miserable plight of the twenty million black people in America is the
fulfillment of divine prophecy. We believe that the serious race
problem that the Negro's presence here poses for America is also the
fulfillment of divine prophecy. We also believe that the presence
today in America of the Honorable Elijah Muhammad, his teachings
among the twenty million so-called Negroes, and his naked warning
to America concerning her treatment of these twenty million ex-slaves
is also the fulfillment of divine prophecy. Therefore, when Mr.
Muhammad declares that the only solution to America's serious race
problem is complete separation of the two races, he is reiterating what
was already predicted for this time by all the Biblical prophets. . . .

In concluding, I must remind you that your own Christian Bible
states that God is coming in the last days or at the end of the old
world, and that God's coming will bring about a great separation.
Now since we see all sorts of signs throughout the earth that indicate
that the time of God's coming is upon us, why don't you repent while
there is yet time? Do justice by your faithful ex-slaves. Give us some

land of our own right here, some separate states, so we can separate ourselves from you. Then everyone will be satisfied, and perhaps we will all be able to then live happily ever after and, as your own Christian Bible says, "everyone under his own vine and fig tree." Otherwise all of you who are sitting here, your government, and your entire race will be destroyed and removed from this earth by Almighty God, Allah.

5. Religious Bases for Nonviolent Resistance[1]
✢ *Martin Luther King, Jr.*

Over the past century, the black community in America has found much of its leadership among the ministers of its churches. Little wonder, then, that its struggle for self-realization has been significantly shaped by religious themes and motivations. ■

During my freshman days in 1944 at Atlanta's Morehouse College I read Henry David Thoreau's essay *On Civil Disobedience* for the first time. Here, in this courageous New Englander's refusal to pay his taxes and his choice of jail rather than support a war that would spread slavery's territory into Mexico, I made my first contact with the theory of nonviolent resistance. Fascinated by Thoreau's idea of refusing to co-operate with an evil system, I was so deeply moved that I reread the work several times.

A few years later I heard a lecture by Dr. Mordecai Johnson, President of Howard University. Dr. Johnson had just returned from a trip to India and he spoke of the life and teachings of Mahatma Gandhi. His message was so profound and electrifying that I left the meeting and bought a half-dozen books on Gandhi's life and works.

Before reading Gandhi, I had believed that Jesus' "turn the other cheek" philosophy and the "love your enemies" philosophy could only be useful when individuals were in conflict with other individuals — when racial groups and nations were in conflict, a more realistic ap-

[1] "Martin Luther King Explains Nonviolent Resistance," from the book *Eyewitness: The Negro in American History, Revised Edition,* by William Loren Katz. Copyright © 1967, 1971 by Pitman Publishing Corporation. Reprinted by permission of Pitman Publishing Corp.

THE CONTEMPORARY CHALLENGE: *The religious community could not long remain aloof from the profound changes at work in the modern world. Many responsible religious leaders have sought to alter traditions to meet new demands and to make religious institutions more responsive. Above, Rev. Malcolm Boyd, an Episcopal priest, conducts a workshop in a New York coffeehouse.*

American blacks, from the beginning of their struggle for equality, have drawn heavily on Christian traditions for their inspiration. There are notable exceptions, however. Malcolm X adopted the Black Muslim faith and renounced his Christian name.

This nun in modern garb is one of many who express their religious commitment by working as civilians in a variety of community projects.

proach seemed necessary. But after reading Gandhi, I saw how utterly mistaken I was.

During the days of the Montgomery bus boycott, I came to see the power of nonviolence more and more. As I lived through the actual experience of this protest, nonviolence became more than a useful method; it became a way of life.

Nonresistance attacks the forces of evil rather than the persons who happen to be doing the evil. As I said to the people of Montgomery: "The tension in this city is not between white people and Negro people. The tension is at bottom, between justice and injustice, between the forces of light and the forces of darkness. And if there is a victory, it will be a victory not merely for fifty thousand Negroes but a victory for justice and the forces of light. We are out to defeat injustice and not white persons who may be unjust."

It must be emphasized that nonviolent resistance is not for cowards. *Nonviolent resistance does resist.* If one uses this method because he is afraid, or merely because he lacks weapons of violence, he is not truly nonviolent. That is why Gandhi often said that if cowardice is the only alternative to violence, it is better to fight. He made this statement knowing that there is always another choice we can make: There is the way of nonviolent resistance. No individual or group need submit to any wrong, nor need they use violence to right a wrong. This is ultimately the way of the strong man.

The nonviolent resistance of the early Christians shook the Roman Empire. The nonviolence of Mahatma Gandhi and his followers had muzzled the guns of the British Empire in India and freed more than three hundred and fifty million people from colonialism. It brought victory in the Montgomery bus boycott.

The phrase "passive resistance" often gives the false impression that this is a sort of "do-nothing method" in which the resister quietly and passively accepts evil. But nothing is further from the truth. For while the nonviolent resister is not physically aggressive toward his opponent, his mind and emotions are always active, constantly seeking to persuade his opponent that he is wrong — constantly seeking to open the eyes of blind prejudice. This is not passive nonresistance to evil, it is active nonviolent resistance to evil.

Nonviolence does not seek to defeat or humiliate the opponent, but to win his friendship and understanding. The nonviolent resister not only refuses to shoot his opponent but he also refuses to hate him.

To strike back in the same way as his opponent would do nothing but increase the existence of hate in the universe. Along the way of life, someone must have sense enough and morality enough to cut off the chain of hate.

In the final analysis all life is interrelated. All humanity is involved in a single process, and all men are brothers. To the degree that I harm my brother, no matter what he is doing to me, to that extent I am harming myself. Why is this? Because men are brothers. If you harm me, you harm yourself.

■ *The Student's Paperback Library*

The selections chosen for this book have emphasized narrative, descriptive, and biographical materials. For additional selections more theological in character, you may wish to consult Robert L. Ferm, *Issues in American Protestantism;* Sydney E. Ahlstrom, *Theology in America;* William G. McLoughlin, *The American Evangelicals, 1800–1900;* William R. Hutchison, *American Protestant Thought: The Liberal Era.*

Parallel treatments of the three major religious groupings will be found in Winthrop S. Hudson, *American Protestantism;* John Tracy Ellis, *American Catholicism;* and Nathan Glazer, *American Judaism.*

Two books by Edmund S. Morgan provide a good introduction to Puritan New England: *The Puritan Dilemma* and *Roger Williams: The Church and the State.* Documents on the great crisis of eighteenth-century religion may be found in Alan Heimert and Perry Miller, *The Great Awakening.* The pietistic side of colonial religion is treated in William G. McLoughlin, *Isaac Backus;* the rationalistic side is discussed in Conrad Wright, *The Beginnings of Unitarianism in America.* For a good picture of Philadelphia Quakers, consult Frederick B. Tolles, *Meetinghouse and Countinghouse.*

In the early nineteenth century, Protestant-Catholic relations are dealt with in Ray A. Billington, *The Protestant Crusade.* Mormonism is treated in T. F. O'Dea, *The Mormons;* and an important aspect of anti-slavery is analyzed in Gilbert Barnes, *The Anti-Slavery Impulse.*

After the Civil War, the religious response to the problems of industrial society is discussed in C. H. Hopkins, *The Rise of the Social Gospel, 1865–1915;* and also in H. F. May, *Protestant Churches and Industrial America.* A key issue in Catholic history is the theme of T. T. McAvoy, *The Americanist Heresy in Roman Catholicism.* Donald Meyer, *The Positive Thinkers,* deals with mind-cure religion and related tendencies. One form of black religion is the subject of C. Eric Lincoln, *The Black Muslims in America.* A useful compilaton of court decisions is J. Tussman, *The Supreme Court and Church and State.*

Sociological perspectives on American religion are to be found in H. Richard Niebuhr, *The Social Sources of Denominationalism;* and Will Herberg, *Protestant, Catholic, Jew.*

■ *Questions for Study and Discussion*

I. Errand into the Wilderness

1. What arguments did Richard Hakluyt advance in urging the English government to adopt a policy of colonization in America? What comparisons did he make between the Anglican and Roman Catholic churches?

2. What evidences of Providence did William Crashaw see in the experience of the Jamestown settlers?

3. What developments led the Pilgrims to leave, first, England, and then Holland for America? Describe their preparations for departure. With what feelings did the Pilgrims view the country to which they had come?

4. On what basic principle did New England Congregationalism rest? How did the Puritans and the Pilgrims organize their churches? What were some of the ideals embodied in their church covenants? What procedure was followed in the selection and ordination of church officers?

5. How did the Calverts endeavor to insure that religious toleration prevailed in Maryland? Show how toleration triumphed in the case against William Lewis.

6. How did William Penn's laws uphold freedom of conscience? What was the law concerning the Sabbath? How did Pastorius describe the religion of the American Indians? What were the principal religious groups in the province? How are they characterized?

II. Times of Transition and Tribulation

1. Irrespective of their motives for coming to America, what tasks did the first settlers have in common? Why did Samuel Danforth criticize the Puritan churches? What changes had taken place?

2. Why may it be argued that Cotton Mather's advice to the ministers on the witchcraft question contributed to the eventual decline of witchcraft accusations? What was his advice?

3. What was the position of the Germantown Quakers with respect to slavery?

4. What changes in belief were taking place with respect to men's perceptions of natural phenomena? Who were the "deists"? How did Benjamin Franklin conceive of God? What did he think was proper behavior toward God? What were his views about human pleasures?

171

III. The Great Awakening

1. What was the Great Awakening? How did it come about? What effect did it have on New England? Why was it an important turning point for American religion? Why did Jonathan Edwards feel that "the Spirit of God began . . . wonderfully to work" in Northampton in 1734? Describe the behavior of Phebe Bartlett. Why was it so remarkable?

2. What was Benjamin Franklin's attitude toward George Whitefield's theology? What was his response to Whitefield's orphanage project? Describe the friendship that existed between the two men. What effect did Whitefield's preaching have upon his hearers? How large were his audiences?

3. Explain the difference between Calvinism and Arminianism. How did John Bass come to question Calvinist doctrines? Why did the congregation of his church dismiss him?

4. How does the Reverend Devereux Jarratt describe the effect of revivalism in Virginia? Are there any similarities between revivalism there and in Northampton (described on pages 28–35)? Does Jarratt have any reservations about the quality of the revival meetings?

IV. Revolutionary Times

1. What changes in ecclesiastical institutions were brought about by the American Revolution? How did the Revolution provide impetus for the movement toward the separation of church and state? What were Jefferson's reasons for opposing a state-enforced uniformity of religion?

2. On what grounds did Theophilus Parsons seek to justify government support of the churches? In what respect have Americans tended to agree with Parsons? Disagree?

3. What ties between the Anglicans in this country and in England were dissolved by the Revolutionary War? How does American Episcopal Church government differ from that of the Church of England?

4. How did anti-Catholic prejudice handicap Catholics in England? How was this situation changed for Catholics in Maryland and Pennsylvania? Describe the consecration of the first Bishop of Baltimore.

5. How did Giovanni Grassi explain the growth of religious sects in the United States? How did Americans observe the Sabbath? What did Grassi criticize about the way Americans interpreted the Bible?

V. Evangelical Protestantism

1. Why did spokesmen for evangelical Protestantism encourage revivals? What special kind of experience characterizes evangelical Protes-

tantism? Describe the bodily exercises which accompanied the religious revival at Cane Ridge, Kentucky. According to Barton W. Stone, what were their beneficial effects?

2. What three innovations were introduced by Charles G. Finney at revival meetings? How did he seek to justify each?

3. What role did home missionary societies play in the westward movement? What was the "New Haven Band"? Describe Flavel Bascom's congregation. What style of service did he attempt to promote?

4. With what convictions did Adoniram Judson go to Burma? What expectations did he have? Were they realistic? How did he seek to further missionary efforts elsewhere?

5. What, according to William Cogswell, was the purpose of the various benevolent societies? How was the church compared to an army?

VI. Variant Forms of Dissent

1. On what grounds did some groups disagree with the main thrust of evangelical Protestantism? What did these dissenting groups have in common? How did early Unitarianism differ from orthodox Christians? What was the response of the evangelicals? How did Channing react to their "system of exclusion"? Why did he feel that theological differences ought not to divide Christians?

2. What did Bushnell argue were the best means for developing a Christian character? How did he criticize the belief in sudden conversion?

3. What is the difference between "High Churchmen" and "Low Churchmen" in the Episcopal Church? How was this difference illustrated at the confirmation service described in the selection?

4. How did William J. Mann characterize American piety? How does he describe the strengths and weaknesses of "Puritanism"? What does he think has been its effect upon Methodism? Lutheranism? What course does he recommend for Lutherans?

5. Why were many Americans suspicious of Mormons? Describe the Mormon city of Nauvoo. What happened to it? What was the Great Vase? How does the writer describe the surviving inhabitants? Where did the Mormons go after leaving Nauvoo?

6. What charge was brought against the schoolteacher in *Commonwealth v. Cooke*? What reasons did the court give for dismissing the charge? Does this case bear out the contention of Catholics that the atmosphere in the public schools was thoroughly Protestant? Why or why not?

7. What was the prevailing belief among evangelical Protestants regarding the Jews? How did Rabbi Wise represent Jews at the church gathering he attended? What response did he receive from his audience?

8. How did Chief Red-Jacket describe his people's relations with whites? Why was he skeptical of Christian missionaries? What course of action did he recommend to them?

VII. Religion and the Institution of Slavery

1. How did the spiritual "Go Down, Moses" reflect the plight of Negro slaves?

2. What event precipitated the withdrawal of Richard Allen from St. George's Church? Describe the plans for establishing the first African Methodist Episcopal Church in the United States.

3. What form of religious excitement did Frederick Law Olmsted find on the rice plantation in Georgia? In the church in New Orleans? What purpose do you think emotionalism served in Negro churches? Are there any evidences of racial bias in Olmsted's descriptions?

4. How did James Henry Hammond use the Tenth Commandment as a justification for slavery? What other evidence did he cite from the Old Testament to support his argument? What instance of slavery in the New Testament did he cite?

5. In what respect were many antislavery meetings similar to revival meetings? What topics were discussed by the students of Lane Theological Seminary? What was said about the condition of slaves? What was the outcome of the meeting?

6. What images are found in Julia Ward Howe's hymn? Where did they come from?

VIII. A New Setting: Urbanized and Industrialized America

1. How does the writer contrast the society of his day with earlier periods? In his opinion, what question still occupies the minds of urban dwellers? What new approaches are recommended for reaching the "laboring class"?

2. How did some churches adjust to growing urbanization and industrialization? What was the "institutional church"? What social services were provided by the Berkeley Temple?

3. What objections were raised against Washington Gladden's ideas? How did the facts fail to support them? How did Gladden argue that it was necessary for the church to become involved with social issues?

4. What economic preconditions did Walter Rauschenbusch see as necessary for the establishment of the "co-operative commonwealth"? Did Rauschenbusch approve the principle of monastic withdrawal from an evil society? What alternatives did he propose?

5. Why was the Federal Council of Churches formed? What did its "Social Creed" emphasize?

IX. The Enlarging Pluralism of American Religion

1. How was religious pluralism broadened in the United States during the nineteenth century? To what human concern did Christian Science address itself particularly? How did Mary Baker Eddy explain her discovery of Christian Science?

2. What is premillenialism? Who was Mrs. Ellen G. White? According to her, what are the signs of the second coming of Christ? According to the millenialists' scheme, how and when will the judgment of the wicked take place? How is the final battle between Christ and Satan depicted? What happens to the wicked?

3. How did the Saint Patrick's Day parade illustrate the growing strength of the Roman Catholic Church in this country? How was it received by the people of Lowell? What other ethnic groups arrived? What was the public sentiment toward these groups?

4. What criticism did Archbishop Ireland make of many American Catholic priests? Why was Father Hecker an exception to this criticism?

5. To what does the term "Orthodox Church" refer? Who introduced the Eastern Orthodox faith into this country? Why are Greeks who have settled in the United States unwilling to accept the spiritual guidance of Russian Orthodox clergymen?

6. When did Jews arrive in this country in largest number? Why did Hutchins Hapgood describe the lower East Side of New York as "the largest Jewish city in the world"? How did the older generation of Jewish immigrants differ in their customs and outlook from their children who were brought up in American schools?

X. New Intellectual Challenges

1. What three kinds of response did the Darwinian theory provoke among Christians? How did Bishop Wilberforce, Dr. Hodge, and Professor Duffield attack Darwinism? How were they replied to? How did President McCosh of Princeton deal with the problem? What does Andrew D. White conclude about evolution and religion?

2. How did the critical study of the Bible change Professor Steenstra's views?

3. What new awareness of non-Christian lands did Americans acquire during the latter part of the nineteenth century? How did the World's Parliament of Religions illustrate the new mood?

4. What events transpired at Princeton Theological Seminary which precipitated the establishment of the Westminster Theological Seminary? What is meant by the designation "fundamentalist"? "Modernist"? What was Professor Machen's view of the state of Protestantism?

5. How did Harry Emerson Fosdick's reaction to the theological controversy differ from that of Professor Machen in the preceding selection? Why did Fosdick disagree with the radicals?

XI. Some Recent Tendencies

1. What is the ecumenical movement? What has the Consultation on Church Union tried to accomplish? What are its stated aims? How does the present mood of Protestant denominations contrast with that of the nineteenth century?

2. How has the ecumenical movement affected Protestant-Catholic relations? According to the Decree on Ecumenism, when might Catholics be permitted to take part in religious services with other Christians? What recommendations are made regarding (a) the locale of such services, (b) the format of the service, (c) dress, and (d) participation of the laity?

3. What does Will Herberg mean by the "three different forms of being religious in the American way"? In your opinion, is commitment to democracy an expression of religion? Explain.

4. What beliefs did Malcolm X come to accept concerning the treatment of blacks by whites? What does this selection suggest about the similarities between the religious experiences of blacks and whites in America? About the differences?

5. From what two sources did Martin Luther King, Jr., derive his philosophy of nonviolent resistance? How does he differentiate between active and passive nonviolent resistance? What is the goal of such resistance? Has it ever succeeded?

■ *Acknowledgments*

Thanks are extended to the following organizations and persons for making pictures available for reproduction: The Essex Institute, Salem, Mass., 17 (top and middle); Religious News Service Photos, 48 (middle), 123 (bottom), 139 (middle), 167 (top, middle, and bottom); State of West Virginia, Department of Archives and History, Charleston, W. Va., 48 (bottom); Union Pacific Railroad, 49 (top); California Historical Society, San Francisco, 49 (bottom); New York Public Library, 67 (bottom); the Historical Society of Pennsylvania, 109 (top); the Boston Athenaeum, 109 (middle); Houghton Mifflin Company, 123 (top); Brown Brothers, 123 (middle), 140 (bottom). The photograph of Mary Baker Eddy on page 139 (bottom) is used with the permission of the Christian Science Publishing Society. The cover photograph is by Tim Carlson.

■ *Index*